ALL I EVER WANTED WAS A LOT OF MONEY & A HUSBAND

Instead I got Enlightenment

Catherine Lenard

YOUR HAND'S IN THE INC.

YOUR HAND'S IN THE INC.

P. O. Box 65
Lakeside, Michigan 49116 U.S.A.

Design and illustration by Catherine Lenard

Printed in the United States of America
First printing: 1997

ISBN: 0-9657692-3-2
Library of Congress Catalog Card Number: 97-090275

Acknowledgements:

Thank you to the following sources for their
contributions to the imagery within this book:
*Animals: 1419 Copyright-Free Illustrations of
Mammals, Birds, Fish, Insects, etc.*, Bizzaro Inc.,
The Clip Art Book, The Flim-Flam Shop, *Women:
A Pictorial Archive From Nineteenth-Century
Sources*, and Rachel.

*My heartfelt gratitude to the many friends who
provided a word, thought or an action which
helped make this book possible.*

*A special thank you to Denis Cooney and
Paul Kakuris whose commentary and support
is deeply appreciated.*

Table of Contents

*Dedicated
to those
who are guided
to read this book.*

Prelude

I am periodically reminded that my higher self, a more evolved aspect of self, has a sense of humor. It continually moves me along despite my fondest attempts at going my own way from the viewpoint of an identity that currently answers to the name printed on my social security card.

From the perspective of personality, I haven't always appreciated what I attributed to higher self workings. It ying-ed when I wanted to yang. It said tomato when I desperately wanted tomahto.

I am aware of its presence through nudgings, knowings, and feelings about what to do in a particular moment. Even when I wasn't very aware of its presence, it was in the background silently guiding my life events. Within these chapters, it makes itself known through perspectives I have gained by way of personal experience. I give them to you from my heart, with the intention that you may find a word, a phrase, or maybe an idea that will in some way be relevant to you.

The events that are related are factual; most names have been changed with respect to the privacy of situational co-creators. I share with you a chronology of transformation . . . enjoy!

Introduction

I've long held the belief that spending time for the sole purpose of accumulating an energy called money has to be one of the great wastes of resources known to humanity. Many of us have structured our lives around that endeavor. I didn't want to. The solution, I thought, was to fall in love with and marry a wealthy husband. Preferably one that didn't come with ex-wives and kids. I wanted a romantic partner with whom I could create free flying, unimpeded adventure. The encumbrances of prior obligations or lack of funds didn't fit the glorious technicolor picture I had envisioned.

Throughout the years, with each unrealized dream and broken relationship, the all encompassing, Holy Grail question remained (and remained and *remained*). When would I have the husband of my dreams and the economic freedom and security I wanted? The Quest has faithfully spiraled me upward and outward through unforeseen dimensions into my own unfoldment.

Case in point. Recently I had the choice of staying home to watch Saturday night figure skating championships alone, uneventfully yet pleasantly, or driving the hour and a half distance to Chicago to join friends at a charity benefit. If I motivated myself from the comfort of the couch, the possibility existed to meet someone eligible to date. The thought of the effort required to compose a fabulous outfit, create make-up magic, stop at the local self-serve gas station in freezing temperatures and drive round trip in an evening, felt nearly overwhelming. Being in a general mindset to meet a partner, I put my attention on how it would feel to go and alternately, on how it would feel not to go. Being relatively neutral about both, I momentarily waited for a feeling that would guide my actions. I felt a resounding "Go." With a perception as clear as that I wasn't going to question a directive that could move me toward meeting someone wonderful.

The event was not what I expected. It was more reminiscent of a college kegger than what the sophisticated address belied. I fell into judgment about the benefit organizers and noted the pickings for potential mates felt negligible, downright disappointing. The only redeeming factor of the evening appeared to be "party psychics" who were available for readings in keeping with a Mardi Gras theme. Out of boredom I joined a line for a palmist. I'd had readings before, so it wasn't for an occult "walk on the wild side," just something pleasant to experience as long as I was there.

Ron provided the usual rundown—old soul, Rings of Solomon, mystic, healer, creative, leadership, business acumen, ya daa da daa da. "Turn your hands back to back, please". . . and upon examining the chicken scratch lines. . . "You have two opportunities for marriage." Now here was something interesting.

The following early spring morning was lovely. The sun was shining and temperatures were warm enough to invite sitting outside on the winter-barren deck of my home. Dressed in Sunday morning sweats and perched cross-legged on a pillow, I sipped coffee and enjoyed the sounds of birds waking up the newly budded trees. Reflecting on the evening before, I wondered if I'd been duped by the strong feeling that had said "Go."

I gradually realized that I had been reminded, through the unlikely guise of a party psychic, where I've been and the way in which my life path is emerging this time around. Sharing the insight with a friend who happened to call, I tongue-in-cheek-lamented, "All I ever wanted was a lot of money and a husband and instead I got enlightenment!" The humanity of distilling my journey into a phantom book title had him chuckling and subsequently sparked a passion to create this book. The desires of personality had, once again, served in an unexpected way.

With amusement and appreciation for the exposed ruse, I began tapping out the initial pages of a first draft the same afternoon.

Give it a rest, you old Battle Axe. Just give me what I want!

self

Come . . . there is much to show you!

higher self

5

Chapter 1

Where is your attention, really?

The Playboy Paper (employee newsletter)

The Way I See It feature:

I might possibly gain immortality if I . . .
"Who wants to be immortal—life's a bitch."

Catherine Lenard, Graphic Designer
Playboy Clubs International

Call it a fallback to eight years of suffer-now-party-later
Catholic school. Call it a tribute to being circumstantially
challenged. Call it being in the pay-my-dues phase of
career development in the Big City. However you want
to slice it, I was in a living hell.

I had moved to Chicago after graduating from a
university in Michigan with a degree in graphic design.
Given my midwest background, Chicago was not as
daunting a move as New York or L.A. and would provide
the big city career experience I wanted. Mary Tyler
Moore's "You're gonna make it after all" theme song
paled in comparison to what I had planned. I was dazzled
by Michigan Avenue and silently announced to the world
on the avenue's bridge that I had arrived and was going
to conquer.

By the time I was working at Playboy, three years later, crushing headaches and panic attacks were the experience du jour. I attributed it to the psycho-management umbrella of the late 20th century, stress.

In an attempt to understand what was causing my angst I rewound events since I'd been in the city. Let's see. . . moving to Chicago without knowing anyone, concrete and asphalt lifestyle adjustment, the apartment that was relieved of darkness only when an errant light shaft reflected off the window of a building that was conveniently located three feet away. Nothing elicited a telling response so far. I continued listing. . . the challenge of having glitter sparkle dreams and a barely slide-by-able salary, being unceremoniously dumped by my stockbroker boyfriend of two years, being relieved of my virginity several years before—ah, pay dirt.

Riding back and forth to work on the number 145 bus that traversed Lake Shore Drive, I wondered how and when fellow travelers had their first full amorous encounters. I speculated on the manner in which they would be judged and compared my own experience. "You, well okay, maybe. You, succumbed to temptation. Sorry, not acceptable." Although in my perfectly respectable early twenties, I had remnants of an old thought pattern that wanted to be married *before*. I had seriously let down the part of myself that covertly clung to parochial school ideals.

Relatedly, I'd had an appointment at a downtown hospital in preparation for pregnancy termination. A fated turn of events mercifully revealed there was no need to continue. I was on automatic numb—grateful to have been spared the ordeal, but no less traumatized.

The pièce de résistance, the something that wasn't, couldn't be happening, rounded out my latest collection of adventures. About a year after the stockbroker relationship ended, I met an illustrator I felt wildly attracted to. "Could this be love," I wondered? Almost immediately, a teensy voice presented itself from somewhere in the back of my head. "You're a lesbian," it taunted.

I dated Steve, the illustrator, intermittently for a stormy year and a half. During the course of our relationship the voice hadn't dissipated despite my analytical attempts to understand what was happening. Although clashing viewpoints were regular fare, he encouraged me to seek intervention. Steve had experienced therapy which made it easier for me to endure the feelings of humiliation and defeat that not being able to figure it out for myself evoked. He referred me to the therapist I would visit on a regular basis over the next three years.

In addition to exploring the phenomenon which motivated my actions, I gained an intellectual understanding of my role within family infrastructure. At times I went into the darkness of my being, the hole in the soul. Treading an abyss, I found myself plummeting into an endless primal mouth which gaped in pervasive blackness. On days I was overwhelmed by the mouth, I saw my therapist on an emergency basis.

The voice was not surprisingly attributed to a defense mechanism. It was a way I kept myself distanced from people in an attempt for emotional safety. I was assured it was symbolic. The explanation was plausible; I had sensed the cause, but the experience hadn't been alleviated.

In moments of uncertainty I doubted the wisdom of the therapist. Was she *really* sure about this? At times I would converse with someone, but wasn't really present, in the moment, because I was distraught and distracted that what the voice said was true. When it surfaced I prayed, journaled and attempted to will it away. In moments of courageous overwhelm I allowed the thought of assuming another lifestyle if the action would buy me peace. The voice would ultimately weave in and out of my life to varying degrees over the next ten years. Interesting, this mouth and voice were, considering I had a bonafide fear of speaking out.

GIANT MOUTH DEMANDS ATTENTION—NOW!!

*If your attention
is focused on
"muck,"
is it any wonder
that you
would be
"stuck in the muck?"*

Although I thought I was focused on making a life for myself, most of my attention was consumed by inner demons. I was on a treadmill that looped disturbing thoughts. I didn't have the awareness that: 1) if I kept my focus on those thoughts they'd generate more of the same kinds of thoughts or 2) that I had the ability to step off the treadmill and out of the loop.

Chapter 2

About those fears . . .

Despite the periodic side show within, life went on. I quit Playboy after a year's tenure and went independent in an ignorance-is-bliss decision.

Encountering challenging situations with a host of characters, I experienced rapid growth, both personal and professional. Not easy. Living and working in Chicago became palatable only with frequent respites. I had an unspoken pledge to leave town every three to four months which implied flying to a different environment, one that was natural.

So began a lifestyle of intermittent domestic and international adventure travel. To finance my reprieves I'd enter a womb of sorts, creating and delivering projects. Sometimes working around the clock, I lived and breathed deadlines. Within the goal of eventually having a large design office, I developed into a designer's designer and worked with a list of well-known clients. In the process I learned to weather the dramatic feast or famine swings inherent in the creative business and worked them to my advantage. After a deluge of work, I'd leave town to play and recharge. Worry about getting my next project was reserved for re-entry.

Once I'd learned to ski, the Rocky Mountains beckoned, most specifically Vail. Designer-draped schtick was entertaining, but becoming immersed in the splendor of mountain white and feeling the graceful rhythm of well-executed turns was the real draw. I also became certified to scuba dive, preferring eighty degree, crystalline-turquoise saltwater to the opaque depths of nearby Lake Michigan. The rainbow lush world that existed beyond my limited perceptions of the tropical ocean surface was captivating to behold. Most trips were with groups, which was a welcome contrast to working and living alone.

In between working and traveling, I dated. Each new person rekindled the hope that maybe this was The One. I usually went out with entrepreneurially successful men and had a few long term relationships since Steve, the illustrator, and I had broken up years before. By the time I had reached my late twenties I was somewhere around number 106 on the anything from "lunch to two and a half years" list which was diligently calculated from age fifteen.

At this time I met Peter, a Fortune 500 CEO, at a trendy piano bar in Chicago. He was more flamboyant than what I was accustomed to, but engagingly entertaining. When he called from a plane to ask me to join him for dinner (before cell phones were commonplace), I was impressed, amused and agreed. We had been out a few times when he invited me to see his newly acquired condo in a posh, turn of the century building located on the Gold Coast. It was lavishly appointed and had a wonderful balcony which overlooked the mansion housing His Eminence, the head of the archdiocese of Chicago. We were standing on the balcony when Peter disappeared to use the bathroom. Upon his return we embraced and kissed passionately. When his hand reached a dead end in my surfer shorts, I disengaged.

The evening ended pleasantly enough. That was the last time I saw him.

Early in the morning, three weeks later, I awakened with searing pain in my leg. Somehow I knew (oh, I don't know. . . just a hunch) it wasn't a pulled muscle. Ten days later an annoying version of Cupid's Revenge was confirmed.

Although the situation wasn't life threatening, I was devastated. My doctor, a kindhearted man, brilliant in his field, confirmed that the rare circumstance of hand-transfer was not only possible, but responsible. There was simply no other way.

I toyed with legal retribution, but found the event to be too humiliating and wildly improbable to broach with Peter. My world was shattered. "How will someone love me if I am flawed," were my pervasive thoughts. "How could I love myself," was more accurate. I recoiled into a self-imposed prison.

Thoughts create.

*If your attention remains on
what you fear,
it will eventually attract
the very circumstance
you so adamantly resist.*

Although I put up a competent facade, I was a person
who experienced great fear. I focused it on airline travel
terror, being stuck in an elevator, needing a bathroom
and not having one available, being stalked, not having
enough money and miscellaneous disease. Since my
thoughts were inordinately focused on these imagined
events, I eventually attracted all of them.

Chapter 3

There is more, you are more.

During the same month I experienced something which marked a turning point in my journey.

Within the sanctity of a quiet moment, prior to the drudgery of grocery shopping, I thought about a wonderful friend I had met on a New Zealand skiing trip several years before. At that time I'd been in a between-project lull when I decided to experience a foreign country. Taking a good portion of the funds I had to my name, I signed on for a three-week excursion that would take me halfway around the world. Michael was from Chicago, but had a temporary corporate assignment in Hong Kong as an international sales manager for a furniture company. When we met at a group rendezvous point in Sydney, we clicked. He was unmistakably vibrant, yet possessed an inner stability that made me feel safe. He was also a consummate adventurer. I wondered if I had met my match.

Michael was to permanently return home to Chicago within six months. By the end of the skiing trip he had extended an invitation to visit and explore Asia with him before he returned to the States. During the month since we had said homebound goodbyes at an airport in Fiji (the trip included aprés-ski beach time), I received several letters and an audio cassette detailing his life in China. A week after I received his latest communication, a late afternoon phone call relayed the staggering news that he was dead. Michael died sky diving somewhere off the Kowloon Peninsula. His final letter arrived several days later.

I replayed the tape, sent years before, and listened as he offhandedly mentioned "looking forward to a really great fall" in anticipation of upcoming autumn activities. Hearing his voice and knowing what was to come stirred bittersweet memories and poignant emotion.

Shortly thereafter, as I walked to the neighborhood market, I continued to think about him and the seemingly unrelated concept that most of us use only ten percent of our mind's potential. How in the world would I get to the other ninety percent? I was also dismayed because I no longer had a bedroom. At the time, home office spelled second rate. I'd convincingly converted the bedroom into a second office in an attempt to impress a corporate client who wanted to see my "space" as a caveat to being awarded a large job. The bed was currently stacked against a wall and hidden behind a set of bookshelves; friends were coming by to play staff.

At the store I offhandedly flipped through a magazine and was drawn to an article about a man who had started a major restaurant chain. It told of him sleeping in his restaurant bathroom while he was on his way to major successes. I was inspired and amazed at the coincidence of finding information that offered encouragement. I wasn't the only one sacrificing sleeping arrangements with the notion of building a dream.

I casually walked home thinking about Michael, arms straining with the weight of grocery-filled, cellophane-plastic bags. Within a momentary flash, as time stood still, I felt something indescribable move through my body, out my back, and back through my chest, illuminating me in the process. I felt lit up from the inside out like a halogen bulb. I was amazingly stunned. The feeling was of incredible connection—pure, unearthly, boundless LOVE beyond my wildest dreams. I stood dumbfounded on the street, momentarily frozen, laughing and crying simultaneously. I initially had the sense it was Michael's spirit, but somewhere between heartbeats realized the experience transcended any explanation within my realm of possibilities. For the first time in my life I experienced bliss.

When the sweet light subsided, it felt as if storm-laden clouds had filtered the brilliant sun. I was mystified and joyful, yet felt a sense of loss that such an awesome occurrence could not be a normal state of being. As I regained my ability to move, I continued home overflowing with the excitement of what had so serendipitously occurred.

Who you think
you are
is merely a hint
of what you
truly are.

The white light experience made stunningly real the concept that something much grander exists. Until then, the "something" had been a matter of faith, if not experience. Being able to feel the brilliance that surpassed the restriction of self was a gift beyond words.

Chapter 4

Those blasted lessons.

Once I regained my emotional footing regarding Peter and the balcony debacle, I had a sense there was a relationship between my underlying feelings about sexuality and what had happened. The irony of Catholic indoctrination about unsanctioned union, (although I didn't consider myself Catholic or any other religion by this time) and contracting the unthinkable in such an absurd way—overlooking the headquarters of the Midwest Most High—well, there had to be a connection. I felt that if I could find the emotional root of what caused the physical occurrence, it would be eliminated. I booked a Ph.D. hypnotherapist.

While I was in the reception area waiting for my appointment, I noticed *People* magazine had an article about a company in Dallas that had taken an artist's idea for clothing and marketed it nationally. It was a huge success; the artist became a millionaire.

Earlier in the year, being burned out from the self-employed designer roller coaster, I felt I had hit The Wall. Too much work, no work, waiting for the phone to ring, enduring the "just-send-us-your-stuff-we'll-keep-it-on-file-and-drop-dead-while-you're-at-it" auto-response monologue. I'd lost my tolerance for weathering inconsistencies.

During that time the mailman delivered a copy of *Inc.* magazine to my Lincoln Park home/office which featured a cover story about surfwear companies. It heralded incredibly successful young men who held their board meetings on the beach in Hawaii. Finding their story a refreshing contrast to the button-down work ethic of the midwest, I went on corporate design hiatus. I designed a line of surfwear fabrics with series names including Stellar Fruit and Orpheus. They were innovative; they were outrageous. I was having fun.

I spent a week driving from San Diego to L.A. and back, visiting the companies I'd read about. The designs were given lip service, "Like, uh, these are neat," but nothing tangible resulted. I began to consider it a win if appointments were kept. Seems the surfer lifestyle had its own siesta/fiesta timetable even when housed in fancy corporate digs. Having exhausted my patience and contact list, the project was shelved when I returned home.

A few months had passed since the California trip and although I was waiting to delve into the underbelly of my subconscious, the company in Dallas had presented itself. After scribbling contact names on the back of a business card, I tossed the worn magazine onto a coffee table pile and focused on the purpose of my doctor's appointment.

The puzzle piece of information I eventually received from the hypnotherapist echoed protection from getting hurt. Knowing this intellectually didn't save me from periodic bouts of physical and emotional discomfort.

Six weeks after seeing the *People* article, I flew to Texas and showed the president of the company I had read about my fabric designs. He said, "Love your work, give us a product to put it on." The company agreed to finance expenses. I'd give my creativity. If they liked what was created, they'd produce it.

I was on the verge of fulfilling a long-standing fantasy which entailed creating a product that would: 1) touch people in an uplifting way through graphics that would stir the soul and 2) sell on its own so I'd have income that was self-generating. I wanted off the project-to-project merry-go-round. This was my chance to accomplish both.

For the next two months I was in a state of focused elation, literally knee-deep in layout paper and art materials. I worked tirelessly and developed an innovative retail concept including a line of casual classic clothing, accessories, paper products, store design, marketing positioning and strikingly packaged merchandise prototypes.

I gave my presentation three times to the top executives within the company, drawing congratulations and applause. Staff said they looked forward to our imminent working relationship. Having been told I would be contacted shortly, I flew home triumphant.

Weeks went by. Numerous phone calls were made to Dallas, but none were returned. I finally sent a window shade on which my phone number was written, billboard style, with orange fluorescent paint, to the head of the company. He returned my follow-up call and said, "Great shade. Oh, and about the project, well, we (hem) know you can do a few designs, but how (haw) do we know you can do more?" Dreams puddled into a wash at my feet.

Once I'd recovered, I copied a list of domestic retail manufacturers and distributors gleaned from the local library and contacted every company I felt might have an interest in producing the line. The more congenial ones sent ThanksButNoThanks letters.

*Frustration
and disappointment
are tools for your
own growth.*

*Step back and
ask yourself
what you have learned
in the process.*

I set aside corporate design because I thought I was having an emotional meltdown. The years of rejection inherent in the ongoing process of soliciting projects from clients that were less than interesting had become too great. Although I would have preferred acceptance and approval, I realized that what ultimately mattered was how I viewed myself. For the first time in my career, I knew in my heart that the work I created was beautiful, whether others acknowledged it or not. Additionally, when my design abilities were applied to an arena that brought personal joy, I found renewed energy, if not income.

Chapter 5

Seasons are natural.

Back to the drawing board with corporate design, I was in the middle of working on the production of an annual report (I got the job the bed was stacked for), when a friend arrived to help with meals and household details. I was hunched over my drafting table, wrapped in sweat and sweaters, with a one hundred and three degree walking pneumonia fever. The project had a merciless deadline. She marveled at the fact that I would appear to be just short of the walking dead until it was time for a meeting, then—ShowTime. I'd go into the bathroom ala superman, do my thing, and emerge DynamoWoman! After the meeting, I would return home, unobtrusively reinstate my sweats and collapse onto the couch.

It was an allegorical example for my practice of routinely switching back and forth between inner and outer worlds. Generally speaking, I would have preferred a sanely paced, steady flow of projects, but as long as I had cash in reserve and down time, I worked on myself. As I had begun to feel the constriction of increasing emotional discomfort, it became more productive than playing futile phone tag with the middle management "just send us your stuff" monotones.

In an attempt to alleviate the feeling of an unexplained, gnawing fear, I journaled consistently, read books on personal growth and spirituality, meditated and combed over personal history looking for keys to deliverance. Although I had an intellectual understanding of past events, what I didn't know is that long dormant feelings were beginning to surface.

In outer realms, with hopes for extraordinary income extinguished after Texas, my goal for working was to be able to support myself well enough to have money to pay expenses, afford travel, and be in a place to meet a man I would fall madly in love with and marry. I'd continue working for discretionary funds, but he would cover expenses. He'd also have a nice reserve so we'd be able to do whatever we wanted. And if he was a pilot (with his own plane, of course), so much the better. In my universe, travel equated to freedom. The ability to alter destinations on a moment's whim represented the pinnacle of liberation.

Not at all costs, though. I dated a brilliant lawyer who proposed marriage over a lavish dinner five months after we met. He was wealthy, accomplished, and already married (to his practice). He wanted to fly, post dessert, to Las Vegas where he would charge our wedding to his Gold Card. I cared for him, but ultimately didn't feel he was The One.

*Your existence
contains cycles.
Seasons for activity,
seasons for pause.*

*When you flow with
what feels intuitively correct,
despite outer appearances,
know that you are on course
with your life's purpose—
even when it feels like you
don't have one.*

It seemed as if everyone I knew was moving consistently
forward with their lives while I was left to flounder. I felt
terribly inadequate in comparison and pondered the fact
that when Life Plans were dispensed, I somehow missed
the boat. I had no idea that those feelings were my path
for the moment. Although I had thought "real paths" followed a neat and clean script, it was a relief to finally
realize that whatever I was doing or whomever I was
being was The Plan.

Chapter **6**

It's his fault.

Craig called after he saw my picture and write-up in a local newspaper as one of Chicago's most eligible bachelorettes. When the relationship with my lawyer friend was waning, I anonymously entered myself in the competition after seeing a call for entries. While the newspaper's receptionist was momentarily away, I sneaked an envelope with my picture and letter of recommendation onto her desk. The motivation was to connect with my soul mate. I hoped he would find me if I was in a newspaper.

Somewhere in the morning
you came to me with a
RRRing
that smooth and beautiful
airline pilot voice

Coffee #1
Coffee #2
jazz in the park

Pinot Noir, an untried glance
a distant, now happening
remembrance

Fast forward
Fast back
spinning, dizzying calm

Release and repose
a delicate unraveling
spoken and unspoken dreams
unconscious map for traveling

Circumstances, perceptions
gossamer fragile wing
who are you that I now choose
Revealing

Not long after we met, I asked Craig to join me at my apartment because I had questions. He sat on the couch, I sat in an office chair wearing black boots reminiscent of the Third Reich. I held a clipboard in my lap and faced him squarely wearing a black witch hat. It was Halloween and I wanted to add levity to the task at hand.

"Okay, uh, why'd you get divorced, how come you drive your mother's car, why are you living at home, is that a real Rolex, what about this custody thing (he had a young daughter) and do you like to take vacations?"

I had long since grown weary of the getting-to-know-you replay and was going to make sure if I spent any more time with this person, he was someone I wanted to spend time with. Craig was a good sport and encouraged me to ask all the questions on the clipboard list.

I had reservations about his situations (forget the plane, he didn't even own a car), but fell in love with him anyway. Despite the cosmic joke, I hadn't experienced feelings to the degree I had for Craig since the rush of first love at age sixteen. I wasn't going to let glaring red flag details get in the way.

As months went by, The Voice that had initially surfaced with Steve so many years before returned with a vengeance. If relationships bring us into awareness of our healing needs and blocks to love, Craig was a bingo. Despite years of self-work, emotional buttons were pushed I didn't know existed.

Part of me felt very secure with him. I was comfortable enough to discuss any subject, safe enough where sequestered feelings that were awakened by events between us began to leak out. He had a nurturing quality that fostered disclosure. It was in sharp contrast to the "gotta go" facet that periodically exhibited itself, particularly if there was a choice to be made between his daughter and me.

As a young person in serf roles, my childhood experiences indicated that adults held the power. It had been my understanding that as an adult I would finally share the number one slot with my significant other. I believed soul mates created a one on one paradise for themselves.

There was one hitch. Craig was a committed father, had custody of his daughter nearly every weekend and nothing impeded that commitment. This translated into our relationship existing primarily between Monday and Thursday—days that were usually reserved for work, evenings that were time-ceilinged in preparation for the following day.

Although Craig presented many restrictions including his living situation and money issues, I thought I could make allowances for love. But the fact that he chose to exercise father/daughter priority in a steel reinforced, prime-time triangle nearly had me unglued. All the years to find love and now *this*? I was emotionally splayed.

One event in particular stands out. About two years into our relationship we went away together for the first time. Since Craig's financial precariousness had not improved since we'd met, I agreed to split (ugh) expenses to make the weekend happen. We drove to northern Michigan where I showed him favorite places from fond childhood memories. It was a wonderful weekend trip marred only by the fact that we stopped to pick up his daughter as we made our way back into the city. As I sat in my car, his ex-wife (whom I had met once) blind-sided me like a freight train and yelled about why we had gone away when child support hadn't been paid. Welcome home.

Two weeks later Craig told me he was returning to the area we had just visited, this time with his daughter. The information about this spontaneous excursion was flowing from the mouth of a person who had been chronically unable to travel since we had met. He had rented a car, was taking time off from work and arranged lovely accommodations for the two of them. They were leaving the next day. When I voiced disbelief and anger, he spewed, with the narrowed eyes and very strange lips of a provoked animal, "I don't need this," and stalked away.

Thinking about the two of them playing in the sanctity of my shared memories unleashed a spleen-busting rage within me that boiled up from a cellular level. I felt I had one of two choices: 1) pull out an Uzi, or 2) book myself into a padded cell. I was overwhelmed to the degree that I wanted to assume a straddle stance and water the floor. I called my therapist from years before. She assured me that I wouldn't act on the feeling because it was transient. Even so, I neither wanted nor felt I could privately contain my emotions.

Through what I attribute to grace, I vaguely remembered hearing someone talk about a support group for professionals where personal issues were freely discussed in a safe environment. I found a nearby group and attended a meeting that night.

Over the months, where intellectual understandings of years past left off, feelings flooded forth. In the supportive environment of co-journeyers, the impact of ancient events unfurled like a leaf to the sun.

Sometimes those that
we judge as our
worst enemies are
helpmates in disguise.
They show us where
we hurt, which provides us
with an opportunity to heal.

The healing occurs when you
allow yourself to feel the
original pain.

*The rage I felt toward Craig had little to do with Craig.
His actions touched upon deeply buried emotions that
were subsequently brought to the surface. I wouldn't
have believed that statement in the heat of feeling the
feelings that emerged when "he did what he did to me."
I attracted the outer situation because it was time to
release the pain of the original situation. Upon its dis-
charge, whatever it was, became a non-issue.*

Chapter 7

As a prairie is burned back to permit new life, the following year was my season for going to ground zero.

My first car, French, had been purchased from a dealership in an elite North Shore suburb several years before. There were problems immediately, and having repairs done under warranty had become a second career. In a dealership that catered to clientele that would rather bend over, shall we say, than create a scene, I learned to become comfortable verbalizing well-documented complaints.

The latest round of problems entailed exhaust and burned smelling anti-freeze fumes which had been intermittently ongoing for months within the cabin of the car. Craig had the manufacturer's rep involved, but the issue remained unresolved. As unsatisfactory repairs mounted, we began to direct the dealership toward which parts to examine and how to repair them via manufacturer warranty bulletins supplied by a friend. In the meantime, I was developing a weird intolerance to chemical smells including exhaust, dry cleaning fluid and household cleaners.

After driving the car for a short time, I would sometimes experience bizarre symptoms including headaches, dizziness, a burning feeling in my lungs and a strange sensation that felt as if my nerves were stretched and going to jump out of my skin. Being my only source of transportation, I continued to use the car, but kept the windows and sunroof open despite winter temperatures.

During the holiday season I was driving home from the health club after experiencing a rejuvenating work-out. A half hour later I was slumped on the floor of a 7-11 convenience store waiting for an ambulance. My clothes reeked with a toxic, burned smell that had suddenly clouded the inside of the car. I was disoriented and in bad shape. Once in the hospital, the emergency room physician ran a carbon monoxide test (negative), administered oxygen and told me to have my vehicle repaired.

After another stint at the dealership, the car was ceremoniously proclaimed fixed. Having somewhat recovered from the physically weakened state the 7-11 incident had left me in, I planned to attend a holiday dinner at my aunt and uncle's house, a four hour drive away. I didn't want to be conquered by the fear of what amounted to be so many pounds of bent metal. I decided to trust that whatever was wrong had finally been corrected. It would prove to be a mistake.

By the time I arrived, my scalp felt as if it was on fire, my skin was burning in the manner of a severe traveling sunburn and the nerves-jumping-out-of-my-skin feeling was acute. I was subsequently in bed for a week severely reacting to pollutants as minor as the smell of wood burning in a distant fireplace which I detected through a bedroom window that was slightly ajar.

My uncle examined the car and found a fresh pool of anti-freeze that had leaked onto an area of the engine block and a pipe for a heater hose the dealership hadn't bothered to attach. The thought of eventually driving home was frightening under the circumstances, but I affirmed that with the Band-Aid adjustments he made to the areas in question I would be able to endure the trip.

Having made my way back to the city without incident, I went to see my internist. He diagnosed the symptoms as a toxic reaction, but wasn't able to provide more specific information. Returning home, I was again overcome by a rush of fumes in the car and landed back in the emergency room. The most insightful advice I was given was to get the car fixed.

By this time I was in serious trouble. My skin continued to burn, my muscles ached excruciatingly, and I literally couldn't breathe if I came into contact with anything remotely chemical in the apartment including unscented bath soap. Numerous calls to hospital allergy departments and specialists provided no clues into what was happening or more importantly, how to ease it. In physical misery and mental anguish, I made peace with death. I didn't care. I was too exhausted.

By the time several weeks had passed, I had gained enough strength to go to my office (now housed in commercial space) for brief amounts of time. To minimize physical distress, I kept a conspicuous damp wash cloth over my nose and mouth to shield myself from the fumes inherent in navigating through the heavily trafficked city.

Having had more repairs since my latest hospital visit, the car was once again returned by the dealership. As Craig was scheduled to pick up his daughter for their usual weekend visit, he volunteered to test drive it the hundred mile distance the trip entailed. Hopefully he would confirm the fume problem had been resolved. I went home early to give him the keys.

That afternoon I watched the television news which reported headlines of disaster somewhere near downtown Chicago. A story was developing about gas explosions with fatalities. As news cameras panned the blighted area, I suddenly recognized my office building. In disbelief, I called workplace neighbors who confirmed that furnaces had caught on fire which in turn had set off the sprinkler system. From office windows they watched as area buildings burned. Offering to check my space, they called back minutes later to say water was seeping out from under the locked door.

I laid on the living room floor shaken, not only with the stress of another calamity, but in amazement that I had been spared being there that afternoon. The furnace room was located directly across from the entrance to my office. Its door had exploded open when gas surged throughout the building.

The next day I visited the site with Craig. Gas trucks littered the surrounding streets and insurance people tromped through building debris. There was substantial water damage to my possessions and the workspace itself. Moisture clouded the windows, pictures on the walls had curled and bled, and the carpet released a watery squish with every step. My concern was how I would have the stamina to deal with the multitude of details a catastrophe evokes.

At the beginning of the workweek I returned to begin sorting through the soggy aftermath. Synthetically scented disinfectant had been sprayed on wet carpet throughout the building which made it difficult for me to remain in proximity due to brain fog—the feeling of major disorientation and a host of other symptoms that even minor exposure to chemicals continued to trigger. I endured being in the office long enough to meet an insurance adjustor and then tried to reach Craig from a pay phone located across the street. It was rumored gas was again leaking. I felt sick, was overwhelmed and needed a friend.

By late evening I still hadn't located him after exhausting all the usual possibilities. I was concerned. Finally, an operator-assisted late night phone call revealed his whereabouts as I tried to grasp what he was saying. . . Something about trumped up charges for something about taxes mandated by an overzealous prosecutor, instigated by his vindictive ex-wife. It could take months to unravel; he'd be incommunicado. *What?*

After the initial shock of the call, my emotions ran the gamut from deep concern for him to anger at his omission. I'd had no forewarning. He had explained that he'd known about the possibility for months, but with the extreme circumstances I had been under didn't want to alarm me because he wasn't sure the situation would manifest. Feeling betrayed, I neither heard nor understood his logic. The unexpected news was a sucker punch that sent what was left of my world reeling.

At that point in my existence I was basically allergic to everything and no one could tell me why or what to do. My office was a shambles, the car useless. I had no transportation, wasn't able to work, money supplies were running low, and my friend and helpmate was gone. I was alone. In addition, the emotional issues that had been awakened months ago were back burner demons that incessantly licked at my heels. I was only able to give them attention when they rose up and screamed because maneuvering through a day had become an exercise in navigating through a prioritized minefield.

Although life had become an episode in the Twilight Zone, I had to believe there was ultimately a positive reason for the relentless course of events. I had the sense of being tempered through a crucible, for a yet to be revealed purpose.

*When it is time
for change,
circumstances will
manifest to
support that change.*

*Some beings
require more drama
than others.*

Whatever thoughts I had about the way things "should
be" were forever altered. I learned to operate on a
moment to moment basis because that was the only
way it was possible to function. The word "function"
took on new meaning as well.

Chapter **8**

Your white-knuckle grip
is optional.

Years before I had purchased a book on inner healing. In my current state of affairs I found a particular section that provided comfort. It was about a process mysteriously referred to as chemicalization which, given my situation, held a particular irony. The idea was that when new thoughts, ways of being, are introduced into an old mental framework, chaos ensues until the new thoughts take hold. It's metamorphosis. The author assured that everything going wrong at once was actually a good sign, to hang on. When the upside down righted itself, life would be much nearer to one's heart's desire. In light of what had occurred, I figured things were on their way to getting *really* good. The chapter was dog-eared; it helped keep me afloat.

During that time I began attending a progressive, nondenominational church. Acquaintances had recommended it, finding the services relevant and uplifting— a haven for traditional religion dropouts. I found it provided a positive take on "church" and the warmth of its congregants to be a welcome oasis. In addition, interesting speakers were an ongoing event.

When I heard there was to be a talk about nutrition and physiology presented by a man from a health institute in Florida, I made plans to attend. Finding his knowledge impressive, I asked if he had any information about what might cause the burning sensation that had continued to travel from the soles of my feet to the crown of my head since Christmas. He suggested heavy metal toxicity as a strong possibility. I staggered with the impact of the information—in despair at how damaged my body could be and also with anger directed toward those who maintained there was nothing wrong with the car.

Struggling to understand the cause and effect of my body's haywire condition, thoughts vacillated between the strange symptoms that continued to present themselves to possible unseen reasons for their appearance.

Through the support group I attended, I heard someone mention that they had received a session from a MariEL® healer.[1] The technique involved healing work on dimensions other than face value physical and emotional. This intrigued me because in addition to everything else that needed resolution, The Voice was persisting as part of the back burner demon crew that demanded attention. I wondered if there was something causing the phenomenon that traditional healers weren't aware of. In an introductory talk I attended, the practitioner explained that MariEL healing worked with the highest forms of energy, including angelic. These energies helped access and release emotional pain that was stored in the body. Sure, why not.

Denis gave a demonstration focusing MariEL energy with his palm. Although I felt the presence of a holy man, I attempted to bounce back whatever he was directing rather than hold him in guru-ed esteem. Whatever that exchange signified, provided the basis for our relationship. Thereafter we met twice a month for sessions—he, I and the ever present angels. The terror in my eyes that had risen over months of trauma and

1. See Appendix.

the tortuous voice that had persisted for almost a decade mercifully began to fade.

In the aftermath of events, I moved my office into what had been the small bedroom of my apartment; what didn't fit was put into storage. The car was not fixed. I calculated that I could physically withstand being in it for nine to eleven minutes with all the windows open and the familiar wash cloth over my face. With this adaptation, I was able to drive the few miles to church or six blocks to the grocery store. Other than that, I used public transportation or rented cars when necessary requesting non-smoking vehicles that hadn't been doused with disinfectant.

Eventually a clinical nutritionist was found who was familiar with my physical symptoms. She directed me to tests that confirmed heavy metal toxicity and subsequently prescribed a detox cleansing regime which included a strict diet, sauna, exercise and nutritional supplements. Craig had returned from his "digression," but our relationship was more off than on. I had a few small design projects, but most of the year had been spent reassembling the shattered pieces of what used to be my life.

After months of documentation and legal strong-arming, a settlement was received on damages to my office from the gas company. In addition, a law suit was filed naming the two automobile dealerships that had serviced my car and its Frog manufacturer as defendants.

Around Christmastime, almost a year to the date of my first emergency room visit, a longtime friend sent an airline ticket so we would have the opportunity to visit in Arizona. During that week, I took time to spend a day alone in the red rock beauty of Sedona. I awakened early in the morning and went to Bell Rock. Sitting in the cold, clear stillness, I found myself inadvertently rotating from the waist up in a meditative state as coyote calls echoed off nearby canyon walls. At the time, I didn't know that vortex, within the context of Sedona, was synonymous with energetic whirlpool. I was intuitively in touch with the phenomena that was intrinsic to the area.

Hearing of the experience, Denis suggested that kundalini energy was awakened within me. He felt I had become grounded enough to experience it. From what I could gather, it meant I'd have a different way of looking at things—more wisdom, light and love.

*When you begin
letting go
and learn to relax
into the moment,
you will begin to feel
the gentle support
that was there
all along.*

I was beginning to get an inkling of "flow," which I
defined as the feeling that every move I made didn't
have to be calculated. There appeared to be a margin
for error. Since I had never trusted the world and felt I
needed to control it or suffer excruciating consequences,
this was a revelation. I allowed myself to acknowledge
only a smidgen of "flow" in case it wasn't really true.

Chapter 9

**Do you say what you want,
do you want what you say?**

The following year I read every self-help and spiritual book I felt attracted to, sometimes devouring three at a time. I regularly attended classes and lectures on topics of the same nature and participated in personal growth seminars advancing to the leadership level. I continued with MariEL work, had bodywork sessions, joined growth-oriented discussion groups and connected with mystics and psychics. Plumbing my own depths, I vowed to rip out by the root anything that held me back. Some days were jubilant with moments of elation, other days I was sure I wanted to die.

Craig used to harangue me about "becoming whole," not looking for someone else to fill in the missing pieces. Through the inner work I had done since meeting him, I knew this was true. In a moment of post-lover conciliation, he acknowledged the progress I had made on my journey. He remembered, with tears in his eyes, that through great turmoil I hadn't given up, hung in and kept fighting. Those of lesser determination surely would have thrown in the towel or permanently crumbled. He congratulated me on becoming whole.

There was great balm in those words since I had taken his former viewpoint to heart as a criticism and reason for him not wanting to freely spend time together.

Events unfolded. I secured a prestigious design contract with a major publication, traveled to Vail on a group ski trip and spent a week at an out-of-state environmental health clinic for documentation and diagnoses of the chemical sensitivities I was still experiencing. After being probed, stuck and gassed, I had confirmation of chemical allergy for my lawsuit. I also became bored with print design and decided to make jewelry.

Craig and I had gone to an art show opening in the city's River North area. We nearly tripped over a young man with angelic countenance who was crouched on the street selling heart-shaped pendants embellished with a cross. Touched by the subject matter, I purchased one. Days later, I was inspired to create my own.

Playing with clay and non-toxic, meldable plastic was a nice change of pace. As I worked with the elements of color and design, several patterns within the heart/cross motif emerged. I excitedly experimented with the new materials and put the first prototype into the oven to bake. When it unexpectedly fell from a rack, I automatically grabbed it without protecting my hands. I burned my left ring finger and soothed it with ice for several hours. When the ice was removed, a blister appeared in the shape of a heart with a cross in the center.

My friend, Merrill, a renowned psychic type, felt that the designs that were created were extremely powerful, even mystical. He said they held their own knowledge and transmitted information.

Once again, the dream of being able to combine design work with something that had an uplifting affect on people which resulted in a self-generating business coursed through me. This idea was blessed, ordained by the cosmic. It *had* to work. I had a blister for pete's sake! I had visions of hiring mentally challenged individuals to assemble the pieces and saw them happily immersed in working with message-laden shapes and colors. A successful, love-fest business, right down to production.

A few were sold—the individuals who purchased the pendants were aware of their value. They had the attention of a known fashion designer who considered them collector's items and suggested marketing possibilities. When I subsequently made the buyer rounds to small boutiques and larger stores including Henri Bendel and Bloomingdales, there was no interest. Needing to earn a living, I again focused on corporate design.

In the personal arena, my own healing continued. I had a significant realization that painful experiences were challenges to grow through. They had actually served, because in the process of working them through, I learned a great deal about myself and what I believed. It became evident that I had judged myself harshly (understatement) and resisted the life experiences that weren't favored. As a result of newfound awareness, a softening occurred. Reaction to trauma yielded to an innate self-confidence. On a profound level, I knew if I could survive everything that had happened so far, I could handle anything. Relationship with myself improved.

I have outstretched arms with golden streamers lofted, trailing . . . free

46

On an early spring Sunday afternoon, I went to the Art Institute. I wanted to be around people and have the opportunity to meet someone to date. Tired of my somewhat cloistered existence, I untypically donned a short skirt, sweater and heels. Denis suggested that what one puts out is what one attracts. If I put out physical attraction, then guys interested in sex will respond. I felt he was being somewhat extreme in his interpretation of a short skirt, but interestingly enough, having been in the same mindset two days earlier, I had unexpectedly heard from Tom, a handsome Canadian(eh) entrepreneur (divorced, two kids) I'd met in Vail nearly a year before. Two weeks after our initial meeting on a chairlift, we'd had an interlude in Chicago when he was in town for a business conference.

We had barely been able to contain ourselves during dinner in a corner booth at Shaw's Crab House. Escalating magnetics pulled us increasingly closer between salmon and chardonnay. A delicate salad of ephemeral greens took on the flavor of cardboard. Between bites, pants, and swallows, I feebly joked about being under the influence of a Venus brew of endorphins and pheromones. We were at the effect of logic-numbing chemistry and looked upon one another as if we'd been left in the drooling aftermath of a stun gun. The awareness didn't dilute the feelings.

After dinner, we floated toward Michigan Avenue pausing on a stairway to recklessly delve into a passionate kiss. Seeing that my lipstick had stained both of our faces red from nose to chin, we stopped at my health club, which was conveniently located at the top of the stairs. We ducked into an obscure ladies room and cleaned up, taking a detour into one of the stalls. Seeing us leave in a cloud of our own making, a wisecracking cleaning woman, with a twinkle in her eye and a grin on her face, teased, "Well, I hope you had a good time!" I was deliciously lost in the excitement of possibility.

Eventually long distance communication dwindled to nil. Since we hadn't had any contact for months, as far as I was concerned, Tom's international statute of limitations had expired. The last time we talked he had mentioned conflict between his feelings for me and a woman in Canada. Canada had won out for the time being. When he unexpectedly called eight months later, I was playfully guarded.

"So, why are you calling, you little creep?"(!)

Seems he was planning a trip to Vail within the month. He wanted to know if I'd like to meet him, he'd send a ticket, he wanted to have a mountainside "heart to heart." Turns out it was coincidentally the same week I planned on being in the area with a group. Not wanting to dabble in the assumption hall of mirrors, I cut to the chase:

"So, are you available now?"
"No."
I pressed for details.
"I'm married."
"What?"
"I'm married."
"*What?* You got married since I met you?"
"No . . . I was married."
"You said you were divorced."
"I was . . . a long time ago. Then I got married."

That, as is proverbially said, was that.

"So Denis," said I. "You're telling me I sent signals to Canada?" "Yes," said he. "You're telling me I created five days in Vail at exactly the same time he was going to be there because I sent out some kind of weird inter-country mating signal?" I still wasn't convinced. "Be clear about what you want," he concluded.

I went to see the Monets, but what held my attention was a sculpture entitled *Flight from Pompeii*. It was of lightly colored marble—a woman held a baby, her lover's arm encircled her as he held a cloth overhead as protection from volcanic ash. It was exquisite. What touched me was the aspect of protection. I had been slugging it out for so long by myself I wondered what it would be like to have a man that loved, cared for and protected me. (And sometimes made salad taste like cardboard).

*With
deliberate intention,
you create circumstances.*

*Without
deliberate intention,
you are subject
"to circumstances."*

*I was noodling around with my life rather than taking
command—a little this, a little that. Most of my attention was focused on personal healing, in which I made
great strides. I had ambivalence about my career and
experienced a step forward, step back, but no clear path
of opportunity. I said I wanted a husband, but instead
attracted a very unavailable man. There was a discrepancy between what I said I wanted and what I was
experiencing. The discrepancy needed to be addressed.*

Chapter **10**

Explanations aren't always necessary.

Generally speaking, I was gradually becoming accustomed to unusual occurrences.

Merrill mentioned that an icon of Mary, Jesus' Earth Mother, was reportedly weeping at a local church. As I had heard about similar events for years, curiosity drew me to a west side house of worship. My first impression was that if Mary was crying, it was in response to resident patriarchs. As a prelude to the Viewing of the Icon ceremony, an all male cast took turns solemnly reading from a religious text about harlots and women who needed to be purified.

The Fellini-esque flavor of the moment continued as a procession formed at the back of the church. Religious officials, dressed in black floor length gowns and headgear, tried to contain the crowd as far as maintaining silence. In an oratorical monotone, a baritone voice chastised, "This is the Mother of God weeping. . . the least we can do is maintain silence. I would like TOTAL SILENCE." Which, of course, had no effect on the crowd. Kids were crying and people chatted as Middle Eastern music wound its way through church speakers. It was a controlled, subtle circus complete with candle vendors. I made a purchase and joined the cortege as it made its way toward the front of the church.

As I reached the head of the line, a woman handed me a small plastic bag as a church official dipped a Q-tip in holy water that had been mixed with a drop of "Mary's tears." He made the sign of the cross on my forehead. When I extended my hand to receive the dampened swab, he motioned that it went into the baggie. Apparently Weeping-Mother-of-God-Q-tips were not to be touched by human hands.

Continuing toward the altar, I realized that what was "weeping" was a painting hanging on the wall. I saw water stains that began at the eyes of the depiction of Mary and continued to her chest. It was one of those unexplained mysteries that made life interesting. I was glad to have finally seen what crying icons looked like firsthand.

As I headed east on the Eisenhower Expressway later that evening, the baggie unexpectedly made its point of departure out the open car window into the sultry summer night.

My ongoing chemical detox beverage of choice was distilled water which was delivered to the apartment in five-gallon glass containers. A wooden stand in the kitchen housed the bottle, spares were kept in the pantry. When I awakened one morning and groggily made my way into the kitchen to start a pot of decaf coffee, I was startled to see that one of the spare bottles was placed next to the stand. The hair on the back of my neck stood at full attention as I quickly rewound thoughts. There was no tangible way the bottle could have moved from its position in the pantry the night before. I called several friends in disbelief to share what had happened and Polaroid-documented the stand and spare bottle over the next four days. The bottle changed position three times. I was the only one who had been in the apartment for days and I hadn't moved it. After acclimating to what had occurred and contemplating the significance of water, I felt that whatever caused the bottle to move was ultimately benevolent.

A friend had given me a white and gold colored ceramic angel which sat cross-legged on the windowsill above my bed. It was about five inches high by four inches wide including wings. One morning I awakened to find it in my bed, unmistakably attached to a pillowcase. The fabric was intricately threaded between the arms and legs of the angel dismissing the possibility that it could have been put there in an uncharacteristically fitful sleep. It appeared to be deliberately obvious. I considered it a cryptic honor and left it untouched for days.

Sometimes I had glimmers of the feeling I experienced while carrying the cellophane-plastic grocery bags and the blissful, halogen-white light illuminated me. The feeling occurred randomly in the most usual of situations. I could be actively working through painful emotions or flopped out on the couch, nonchalantly channel-surfing TV. Suddenly I'd experience a warmth and light within my chest that was accompanied by a feeling of pure love. Once it ignited, it was a lost cause. As it had no reason to stop itself, it unvaryingly radiated outward and overflowed through sweet and joyful tears.

*When you allow
events to "be"
rather than demand
explanation or outcome,
you will find a
most delightful
shift in perspective.*

Sometimes you just have to sit back and enjoy the show.

Chapter 11

You will know when you know.

Denis evolved from working with MariEL energy to teaching a powerful self-evolvement course which I eventually decided to experience. Based on the idea that what we believe creates our experiences, the training was to be held at a friend's house in Michigan. So much the better—any excuse to leave the city.

During the weeklong process, I met myself and my own resistances to a degree previously unexplored. I spent a good portion of the time telling Denis and another trainer to "fuck off." At times I saw them through a devilishly pointy-featured filter. Whatever I had brought to the party had put up an interesting fight; my psyche's modus operandi for release was metaphoric kicking and literal screaming. But I kept going. By the time I had finished the Avatar® course, I was on an entirely different plane of existence.[2]

I realized that everything in my experience had culminated in bringing about that moment. All the struggles, pain, disappointments and agony I had endured since moving to Chicago seemed to make sense. There had been method to the madness. I was finally free.

Ah, the Emerald City where I have come to regain my wholeness

2. *See Appendix.*

when the lessons are learned
and the gifts have been given
I will leave this Emerald City
And I, in my wholeness
will return to the Earth . . .

One of my long-standing dreams was to leave Chicago, but I didn't know where to go. I didn't like my apartment and having my office in the bedroom since the aftermath of the gas explosions had grown cramped and tiresome. My bed was in the living room and the living room furniture was in the dining room. I had never owned a dining room table because space requirements for a home office had always taken precedence over superfluous items like a place to eat. I knew home is where the heart is, but longed for physical space that invited a personal life.

Despite my yearnings, there was nowhere I felt drawn to move to. As my frustration escalated each time a lease renewal came up, it was suggested I hug a tree—stay put until I had a clear knowing about where to go. It's just that I had "hugged a tree" for three years and still didn't know.

I seriously considered moving to Arizona, loved the southwest, but ultimately felt it to be too radical a change to make on my own. I had watched friends marry and move to the suburbs, but knew I wasn't a suburb person. Small towns were appealing, but if they were too small, they lacked sophistication. I had hoped

I'd meet Someone and together we'd choose Somewhere wonderful to be. Someone hadn't shown up yet. I decided that if I wanted change, I'd need to do it on my own. Through all considerations, I eventually decided Michigan held the most appeal. I was familiar with the territory, proximity was relatively close to Chicago, and friends, family and clients would be accessible by car.

The relaxed feel of the area had always been a welcome respite and there was an element of sophistication due to the large number of city transplants and vacation homeowners in the area. It was also located on what I considered to be the "good" side of Lake Michigan, the agrarian side with windswept dunes. I didn't know when I'd move or how it would come about, but I grew solid in the choice. I longed to bid the Emerald City adieu.

*Although you seek
a particular outcome,
learn to trust in
your larger knowingness
that operates above
the desires of self.*

Timing is everything.

The feeling of being stuck in a holding pattern was massively frustrating. I also felt that to make an uninspired move for the sake of breaking a stalemate would not be favorable. I found that the concept of "timing" wasn't based on when I wanted something to happen, rather, on when it felt right. There was a big distinction between the two.

Chapter 12

On a particularly clear evening, I went to the beach with a friend. The night was black and stars were plentiful. As soon as we descended the wooden stairs that led from a favorite Michigan inn to the desolate beach, we noticed a star which appeared to be straight across from where we stood. It was out a great distance over the lake, yet cast a yellowish "moonbeam" on the water. We initially wondered if it was a plane, but discounted the idea when we saw several flying in the distance for comparison.

We had been watching it for a while when another blue-white star trailing a "moonbeam" suddenly appeared in horizontal alignment with the one that had previously held our attention. Moments later, in a split second move, both stars rearranged into a vertical stack. When the newer "star" suddenly disappeared, the original began moving toward us. What appeared to be a pin dot moments before was now a rapidly approaching light beam penetrating the blackness like a headlight. As it drew closer, we saw two large, yellowish, front lights and smaller colored lights at what appeared to be starboard and port. No other shape was visible. It barely cleared the trees that fringed the beach where we stood and made absolutely no sound as it disappeared into the night.

I was amazed, but spooked. The thought of seeing

anything unusual in the sky had given me an uneasy feeling since there had been reports of UFO sightings in the Detroit area in the late sixties. Marsh gas, the papers said. Yeah, right. I had been afraid to look out from the bedroom window at night for fear I'd see a spaceship that wanted to take a small-boned girl child hostage. That early experience seemed to be the root of any heebie-jeebies I was feeling as the lights rapidly approached our position in the sand.

When my friend and I eventually climbed the stairs to leave the beach, a mist blanketed the surrounding woods. It cast a magical tone on what had proven to be a remarkable evening. Concern having given way to awe, I felt I had witnessed something extraordinary and wonderful. Either that or a portable airstrip specializing in aberrant plane landings had suddenly sprung up behind the trees.

The next day I learned there had been recent UFO sightings in the towns of Bridgman and St. Joseph. There had also been national media coverage on spectacular sightings near Holland, Michigan, months before. The area was a veritable hot spot.

Back in Chicago, I happened to tune into a local radio program which mentioned an upcoming presentation on UFOs to be given at the world renowned Field Museum as part of a national awareness week. In light of recent experience, definite plans were made to attend.

The speakers held a stellar list of credentials having come from elite scientific and military backgrounds. Their presentation ran the gamut from the much speculated upon Roswell incident of the 1940's to allegations that the government possessed videotape of recent extraterrestrial meetings. They related incidents of military headquarter sightings of spaceships flying in formation over Europe in the 1960's and the kind of shocking news that aliens undetectedly walked among us. Event documentation had been covertly relegated to government files with the James Bond-like designation "Cosmic Top Secret Clearance."

The speakers continued their presentation by showing visual examples of disk-shaped objects that appeared in the skies in art throughout the ages and relatedly addressed the phenomenon of lenticular clouds. It was their opinion that these clouds held a dual purpose, sometimes serving as masking for larger "mother" ships. I'd remembered seeing that type of cloud while skiing in Colorado and driving through the Arizona desert because of its unusual, lens-like shape. If there was more to them than face value, I figured anything with the apple pie designation, "mom," couldn't be all that bad.

A closing prediction was made regarding an acceleration of extraterrestrial-oriented programming in television and media as preparation of the general public for events to come. It occurred to me that Star Trek, by now a cultural icon, was likely a forerunner of the process. I drove home with my hand on the wheel, but my mind racing at warped speed, light years away.

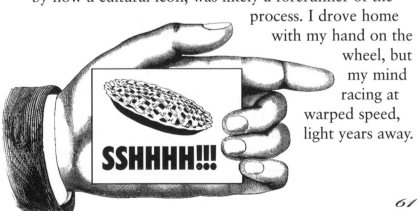

SSHHHH!!!

Life exists
in many forms.

The idea that life existed apart from the earth experience
was initially startling, but vaguely familiar. The fact that
the media often portrayed the concept as something sin-
ister seemed to be another control device that furthered
a stark departure from the wondrous truth.

Chapter **13**

Mindset affects decisions.

That summer I decided to become qualified to teach the course Denis taught. I loved the materials and saw the profound transformation that occurred in myself and others. Wanting to share what I had learned, becoming a trainer would provide a way to interact with people on an intimate level. Personal growth adventures had prepared me well—I'd been there, done that, had gotten multiple t-shirts and lived to tell about it. It would also be a way to earn a living apart from the erratic nature of the design business (sigh).

When I arrived in Florida where the training was to occur, there was a minor glitch. I had checked my voice mail from the airport moments before boarding a four o'clock flight on Friday afternoon and received a frantic message from a client saying she needed something completed for Monday. I had been paper-trail clear that I wasn't available for the duration of the course. Her response was that she didn't know that meant my one-person office was closed. Duh. The corporation had a reputation for erratic managerial behavior, but this one corked it. With vestiges of authority issues dancing in my head, I gave the client the benefit of the doubt and scrambled. I'd explore which beliefs caused the predicament later.

For the time being, I went into hyperaction, sizzling the plastic on my long distance calling card until I was able to devise a plan to get the situation handled. My landlord became available to open my apartment to a freelancer who became available to access the labyrinth of client files in the bedroom/office during an appointed Sunday night computer mega-session. With the phone cord stretched under a hotel bathroom door so as not to disturb a sleeping roommate, I long distance design directed from memory until dawn. My full attention was back on course by breakfast.

I met David when he approached me as I looked out from a conference center window. He was Brazilian, currently lived in the States, and formerly owned a travel company. He had suggestions for perspective expansion. Interesting foreshadowing. Within days I told him I loved him, which was no infatuatory joke. We had an overwhelming connection and I felt as if I'd known him forever. Shortly thereafter I met Jim, a midwestern aeronautics engineer, whom I then introduced to David. There was a profound bond between the three of us that defied logic.

Having foregone his usual profession years before, David was known in spiritual circles for his extraordinary abilities while Jim had spent a lifetime studying metaphysics. Both had the ability to access "timelines," which could best be described as a past life indexing system which enabled retrieval of previous life connections with a directed thought. Their information confirmed a multitude of highflying adventures together in varying roles which I intuitively knew to be true. Considering our colorful history from the viewpoint of current life circumstances, it was amazing that we had momentarily reconvened in the same place and time.

The training, which was powerful in and of itself, unfolded. Coupled with the synergy of reunited friends, it was far beyond anything I could have imagined as I'd boarded the outbound flight from Chicago.

On off hours, as we sat together in a nearby restaurant, people often joined us to share information. Conversation frequently expanded from the topic of finding new, "old" friends, into the fascinating concept of lifetimes which extended beyond the parameters of earth, a subject about which David had extensive knowledge. I was intrigued by the fact that he was in regular communication with contacts "elsewhere" and had supercharged vision to tangibly see who or what he was talking with in other dimensions.

Back on course, David and I were listening to a lecture when I intuitively sensed a whirling column of light energy between us. It may have been fortunate if it had blown us in opposite directions the moment it appeared. Instead, it stayed long enough for him to notice, after which time I interpreted it as an unmitigated sign of an "ordained by the cosmic" love connection. When we were together life was extraordinary. The only glaring downfall in utopia village was the fact that he was inconveniently lock, stock and barrel married.

He said that he and his wife were on again, off again and had seriously revisited the idea of divorce prior to his arrival in Florida and our subsequent meeting. In the all-too-mundane lament of the unhappily married man, he related ongoing discord over a sustained period of time. I'd been through the married conundrum with Tom, eh, the Canadian, and was wiser for the experience. Years before I had adopted a black and white policy regarding prior commitments for no grander reason than I had no intention of sharing. Even so, within the equally prevalent, "But This Is Different," common sense disengaged. In the heady atmosphere of remembered connection and expanded awareness, emotional caution flew to the wind. It was with mock temperance that I adopted a wait and see approach as we re-entered our respective worlds.

*Decisions made
in the flurry of strong desire
may not be
the same choices
made from the space
of your own
centeredness.*

Becoming involved with a married man was not something I would have done from a centered point of view.
In the midst of swirling emotions it became easy to step
off the platform of what I thought were my own guide-
lines into unknown territory. At that moment it wasn't
the quiet knowing of something I felt I had to do. It was
a wildly addictive case of the "gottas."

Chapter 14

**The love vibration is more
than a sixties thing.**

Upon returning to Chicago, I was scheduled to appear
for depositions regarding the near-dormant car case.
In ongoing preparation for eventual trial, I had hired
an environmental firm to test and produce a statement
regarding my car. An inch-thick report resulted which
projected chemical exposures at the time of the major
fume incidents to be in concentrations hundreds of
times over acceptable OSHA standards. Coupled with
medical confirmation of chemical allergy, I was validated.
Weeks later, within the parameters of multiple deposi-
tion days, three opposing lawyers played Round Robin
Decimate. The skills I had gained in Florida greatly
assisted in weathering their Miss-Manners-from-Hell
style of interrogation.

On a more welcome note, I received boxes of
information from David and Jim. There were books,
tapes, transcripts, esoteric newsletters—a treasure trove
of expansive material. The content was enlightenment-
oriented, based in love. We called, wrote, faxed and
together planned an alliance devoted to healing and
self-empowerment.

On a personal level, David said he loved me and
that he and his wife were in the process of making a
final decision about whether or not to stay together.
Since I had existing plans to visit friends in Arizona
within the next month, we planned to meet afterward,

intending to pause for a few days in Sedona. Through spending time together we would gain clarity on our feelings and decide what was next. Within the bubble of a self-induced, malingering spell, I was blinded to anything other than the fact that we'd eventually be together. (What can I say, I had it bad).

Craig drove me to the airport as he usually agreed to do if he was available. In our on again, off again friendship we had revisited having a relationship during the previous year. I loved him, but felt we weren't progressing toward marriage. I had been candid regarding my strong emotions for David and the feeling that the trip was something I needed to do. As we made our way toward Midway Airport, he cautioned me about being a lightning rod in a charged situation. When he subsequently became emotional at the terminal, I was puzzled. Craig hadn't breathed commitment for as long as I'd known him and sudden declarations were foreign. In tears after our interaction, I called a close friend before boarding the plane. She was supportive of what I was doing and reflected that it was necessary to find out what was what because life decisions were at stake.

After a brief layover in St. Louis, I waited until the gate was cleared of passengers before re-boarding. I was emotionally exhausted and looked forward to a nap in the seclusion of the back of the plane. Directed to the only space available, I was seated mid-row, facing backwards, next to a strikingly handsome man whom I had earlier mistaken for a hunk film star. So much for sleep.

Conversation revealed he was the head of an Indian tribal council. As we headed west facing east, we had a fascinating cross-country talk, much of which was on an esoteric level. When he extended an intuitive warning regarding the time I was to spend in Sedona, it only heightened my sense of impending adventure.

When we met, David said he felt relieved and happy. He was definitely leaving his wife. We headed north toward Sedona and stopped en route to admire the spectacular desert view. We shared plans for what we'd like to create; a desert healing center in the middle of desolate, rough hewn beauty. With a special partner, the previously abandoned dream of moving west was possible. Anything was.

Upon our arrival, we drove to Bell Rock. I climbed nearly to the top while David stayed at lower elevations resting an injured leg. When I had visited the area two years earlier in clear morning stillness, I had asked for, meditated on, intended my life mate. I was now with David—a long awaited partner, a twin flame soul mate with potentials that far exceeded my conscious dreams. As I gazed across the canyoned vista, I thanked myself, my higher self, my higher higher self and the powers that be that he was manifest in my life. (I told you I had it bad). When I made my way down and returned to where he was stretched out on a pale rust-colored rock, he said being together was the best thing he'd ever done.

We checked into an unimpressive motel which was barely saved by overlooking a picturesque canyon. When I told him I didn't like the feel of the room, he tuned in to the surroundings and quietly chuckled. David said the place was crowded, which he cleared. "There, better?" It was. I didn't push for another source of lodging because it was getting late and I didn't want to waste our valuable time together. No aesthetics and low on the warm fuzzies? Well, okay, it was only for a night and the room had a nice number, thirty-three. Numerologically speaking, a six, the vibration of love.

The next morning I heard a thud from the bathroom. I waited a minute or so before asking David if he was alright. "No," was the pained response—his back had gone out.

Our thoughts were to return to Phoenix for emergency chiropractic care. As the hours wore on, it became evident we weren't going anywhere. Although he had been able to eventually hobble to the bed, David was in bloodcurdling agony, unable to move. Gratefully, I found a chiropractor in the local yellow pages who was willing to make a motel call later in the day. In the meantime, I helped him as much as I could before briefly leaving the room to get a quick breakfast and the ice bag and other supplies recommended by the chiropractor. While eating, I had the disturbing sense that he was dying. When I returned, he said he had deliberated about leaving his body permanently, but decided it wouldn't have been very pleasant for me to come back and find him gone.

I stayed in the room for the balance of the day, doing what I could to make him as comfortable as possible. In spiritual practice David was able to direct energy to others which manifested in spontaneous healings. I initially found it ironic that he wasn't able to do it for himself, but had the sense that he was working something through which was necessary to his own evolution. I focused loving energy on him, but essentially stayed out of his process, allowing him the space to experience whatever it was he needed to experience. I was unequivocally consumed with love for the man to a degree I didn't know existed.

That afternoon David had a pivotal revelation which involved an action from the distant past that had haunted him for eons. After feeling intense emotions of terror and remorse, experience and release, his body relaxed. In a rapidly approaching transcendent state, I mirrored that he had delivered himself from his torment. At that point he became aware of the benevolent presence of other-dimensional beings in the room and called my attention to them.

As I allowed myself to expand in perceptive aware-ness, I was astounded by the overwhelming beauty of what was occurring. We were surrounded. A feeling of beyond-the-beyond love radiated throughout the room. I then saw geometric configurations of brilliant light which were accompanied by what I can only describe as celestial tones. I wasn't seeing and hearing with my familiar eyes and ears, but with a secondary, subtle vision and hearing that registered clearer than my usual senses. I had seamlessly moved into a state of dance-with-the-stars ecstacy. It was awesome.

Within the higher frequencies of vibration, it is possible to experience events that would otherwise remain inaccessible.

At the time, I didn't understand exactly how or why the "other-dimensional" experience happened, but I now know there are magical realms available to those with an open heart. In retrospect, I believe my physical vibration was raised to the point that I was able to perceive other realities. Being in a state of unconditional love and allowance was the key.

Chapter 15

The Hanging Judge.

Susan, the chiropractor, finally arrived in the evening. As David was still barely able to move, she planned to return early the next day to administer another acupuncture treatment.

After she left, as I looked out from the balcony in a moment of quiet appreciation, I noticed twinkling stars in the shape of a question mark. Although we were delayed under challenging circumstances, it was a wondrous time.

In private conversation the following morning, I asked Susan for her unvarnished opinion of David's condition. She felt the actual injury didn't warrant the degree of pain he was experiencing and, in a comment I didn't fully understand, stated, "The energies really want him here."

While David slept, I went to the nearby airport vortex and climbed to a perch where I had a glorious lunch overlooking Bell Rock and breathtaking red canyons in the distance. When a man approached, I asked if he knew anything about the area's infamous energies. He proceeded to explain the electric, magnetic and electromagnetic properties of the five well-known vortexes. I asked if they could have affected David. His answer was yes, but I didn't get a clear response as to how or why.

He said we were currently standing on a male, electric vortex and guided me to a higher elevation where I could easily feel the physical buzz of intensified energy flow. He explained that the male energies had to do with self-confidence, decision making and other qualities that would typically appear more masculine. Before we parted company he mentioned that in the spirit of giving, his wife, Deborah, provided complimentary psychic readings. After a pleasant exchange debating psychic prediction versus self-generated beliefs, I accepted their card noting that I wasn't sure how long I'd be in the area under the circumstances.

Shortly after I returned to our room the phone unexpectedly rang—it was David's more unexpectedly soon-to-be-ex. After hanging up, he explained that he had called while I was away to let her know he was laid-up. Now knowing his whereabouts, she had called, apparently uninformed about the fact that we were together. Feeling like chopped liver, I questioned his integrity in light of our plans together. He said he understood my feelings and that he'd set things straight. Needing to blow off steam, I went for a walk in the late afternoon air.

Susan, back for another round of needles, had David's lower back looking like an pincushion by the time I returned. He had made the call and related that Barb was furious. I was still upset, but we managed to exchange warm glances between three-way banter that made light of his injury as it eased underlying tensions.

It was well after midnight when a jarring blam-blam-blam shook the door. Shaken from a deep sleep, David groggily asked who it was. A controlled voice icily replied, "I-t'-s B--a--r--b." Given his immobility, I had the honor of greeting our guest. As marksmanship was an avocation, this would be interesting.

A profanity-spewing dervish ripped into the room, made cartoon-like by the fact that the onslaught was delivered in Portuguese. In the aftermath of events, the warning I had received during my flight west flashed front and center. So did Craig's comment about a lightning rod.

Still feeling as if I was in the throes of a late-night B movie, I awakened in a Phoenix hotel suite which was larger than my apartment—it had been the only room available at four-thirty in the morning. I made a reality-check call to the same friend I had spoken with outbound from Chicago and then called Deborah in Sedona. By now I was late for the psychic reading which had been scheduled the evening before.

Apparently the fact that I was no longer in town wasn't exactly a surprise. Deborah confirmed that removing myself from the doorstep negativity that had hatcheted through Sedona was a good idea. The dervish was likened to a harpy and she felt it was imperative that David escape her taloned clutches to save himself. She felt our life paths would separate for several months, but join together again. I was comforted. Exhausted, but comforted.

As I sat in the hotel lobby waiting for a cab, a much-too-exuberant clerk insisted upon conversation. I alluded to an interesting evening and limply joked about writing a story. Often I forget that the universe works through the people we meet. Had I been in a place to remember or remotely care about that in the moment, I would have been more appreciative of the card he handed me: *Rubber Chicken; The Humor Magazine for Grown-Ups.*

An old address was scratched out—it was located where David and I had met months before.

Through a stupored gaze directed out the window of an afternoon flight, I noticed a yellow-white whirlwind following the plane. I discounted the possibility of reflection after careful study and observed it with detached interest until my neck began to cramp nearly an hour later. The balance of the journey was uneventful.

Relieved and grateful to be home, I managed to ingest a microwaved bean burrito pried from a freezer shelf. I poured a generous Canadian Club, mixed it with flat 7-Up, drank, and collapsed into bed.

*Your judgements
are your own.*

Whatever high levels I had been functioning on had
rapidly dropped to the basement. I felt angry, sad, hurt,
humiliated, embarrassed, guilty, disgusted, ashamed,
exhausted and finally numb. The emotions I experienced were the result of the way in which I evaluated
myself and the situation. I repeatedly proved to be
an excellent judge and jury and more often than not
hung myself out to dry. Another person may have had
an entirely different response to the same situation.

Chapter 16

It's all about you.

David called several days later. He had recuperated enough to return home the day after I had left Arizona. His wife had requested that we not have contact for two months and he had agreed to appease her. Deborah's prediction came to mind.

A week later I received a midnight fax. David was again laid-up and had written four pages, the essence of which related saccharin reports about Leave it To Beaver life at home. The letter smacked of contrition and felt as if it was written for the benefit of someone else's eyes. If he was again unable to move, I "wondered" how the letter happened to make its way to the office fax machine. Given his compromised state, I considered whether he was being held hostage. "You want something to EAT (wafting a steaming plate of food)? Then write what I tell you. . ."

As I laid in bed that night, emotions swirled with the vengeance of a twister. I was aware of a standing-room-only cast of angelic characters in the living room/bedroom, but their presence didn't eradicate the pain.

As daily routines continued, David was never far from my thoughts. I didn't believe his letter. I talked with Deborah in Sedona. She concurred that he had acted out of guilt, but ultimately would return. I met with Merrill, but he wasn't able to find any evidence of David in my life through his inspection of my palm.

I knew I was playing a game with myself, but didn't want to admit our relationship had funneled down to the standard cliché.

Having heard about our experience, Jim unexpectedly called on Valentine's Day, no less, to relay information about twin flames. He said sometimes they touched, not to stay together for a lifetime, but to act as checkpoints as they progressed in their individual unfoldment. I didn't want to accept that tidbit and wished he wouldn't have called. The conversation would prove to be our last—third dimensional roles we had chosen this time around would ultimately keep us apart.

Despite profound disappointment, I realized I had received many gifts. I'd known a state of unconditional love for another person to a degree I hadn't fathomed possible. Massive psychic expansion had occurred—we'd had one amazing do-si-do with the sky. There had also been the loving support of friends and strangers to ease the way. Although I missed David, I gradually realized our synergy wasn't a prerequisite for accelerated spiritual growth.

Shortly thereafter, in the gentle, twilight state between sleep and wakefulness, I received a concise knowing that I'd honored the promise of a long-standing appointment to be with David in Sedona. In addition to the gifts I was aware of, our interaction resulted in an admission ticket into broader realms of consciousness. Maybe the twin flame check-in Jim had talked about held an element of truth.

No matter how close I thought I had come to manifesting a true partner, I didn't choose to wait on side-lined what ifs as David worked through his own erratic intricacies. I intentionally pierced the bubble and dissolved my feelings for him, emerging from the situation more expanded, positive and confident. When he called to say he was officially staying with his wife, two months after I had last heard his voice, it was a momentary interruption of an evening rather than a devastating life event.

Your spiritual growth
is your own unique process.

Others may serve
as touchpoints,
but every interaction is
ultimately about
your own evolvement.

Although my feelings for David had changed, I longed
for the sweet connection with the universe that we had
experienced together. When our affinity ceased to be,
I initially felt stranded, as if the path to the stars had
suddenly been cut short. That longing, the silence
between the notes, was vital to my own development.
From that place I would learn to more fully access the
realms which David had previously interpreted for me.

Chapter 17

Going up?

In keeping with the promise of new passage, channels were opened which allowed reception of information from other aspects of consciousness. Where I had been previously able to feel presences, I now had the ability to see with the subtle sense vision that was continuing to develop. The forms of the presences appeared to be luminescent, of light. I was able to access this phenomenon after becoming mentally still and choosing to tune into the higher frequency of whatever it was I was tuning into. Provided "they" were in the vicinity.

After completing a substantial design project, I decided to take a break. I felt I was at a crossroads in my life and longed to take a deliberate sabbatical, not the inadvertent kind that happened between projects. In light of the extraordinary incidents I was experiencing, the plan was to trade in my car for a Jeep—excuse me, sport utility vehicle—and drive to the desert where I'd hang out in terra firma splendor and open myself to information regarding what was next. I found a tiny rental house near Santa Fe which would function as a base and planned a solo journey through Colorado, Utah, Arizona and New Mexico. I specifically wanted to visit the remote town of Crestone in the Sangre de Cristo (Blood of Christ) mountain range in Colorado. Rumor had it that it was situated within dramatic geography and had a reputation for interesting inhabitants and visitors of its own.

Although I hadn't seen anything unusual in the sky since the summer before in Michigan, I'd had a recent experience which didn't involve driving to a specific location. I had been at Denis' home when he asked if I was entirely present. I told him, "No," that I was suddenly feeling a little weird. He suggested staying with whatever it was I was experiencing.

Moments later, as I sat in a chair in his living room, I was engulfed in a large column of yellow-white light as multi-colored light shafts filled the room. It was like being at a rock concert. Was it real or was it Memorex? I was still sitting in the chair, but experiencing what I saw and felt on the increasingly familiar level of heightened awareness. The large light stayed with me as I found myself in an environment filled with the luminescent beings. Feeling comfortable with the ride, I entered a state of allowance. Hands were placed on the crown of my head, and crosses were formed on the third eye and palms of my hands. When I became fully present in the room again, I was slightly disoriented, awash in the now familiar feeling of bliss. It was fun.

Addressing more pragmatic matters. . . I wasn't able to sell my car and couldn't find a jeep that didn't induce an allergic reaction (sensitivities from the chemical incident with The French Car were still an issue). I went into a self-serve department store with the intention of a no brain point-and-shoot camera purchase. A month of research and decisions later, I was equipped with a state of the art Nikon with wide angle and telephoto lenses. I sifted through, threw out, sold and gave away fourteen years of accumulated business paraphernalia. What didn't fit into my bedroom office was disposed of. Personal belongings were pared down to items that were regularly used; anything superfluous was given away. I was intentionally creating a vacuum in which to manifest a new life.

Meanwhile, departure dates kept being pushed back until I completely restructured my itinerary. Plans now focused around an appointment in northern California to teach the self-evolvement course I was newly qualified for. Afterward I would explore the Napa Valley and redwoods instead of a desert sojourn.

*Your consciousness
is the eternal part
of you.*

When I initially heard of people having "beam me up"
experiences, I thought it was a rare, but tangible meeting
as in lunch with the Pope. I didn't know that these events
frequently occurred in consciousness, if not physicality.
The dictionary defines consciousness as "a state of being
conscious," which is "having an awareness of one's environment and one's own existence; mentally perceptive or
alert, awake." Learning this distinction made it easier for
me to trust in the validity of my own experiences.

Chapter 18

You always have a net.

The morning after I checked into a rustic resort in the Napa Valley, I saw a man painting a shed whom I recognized from the night before. He had been sitting at the bar of a trendy nearby restaurant, engrossed in something he was writing. While he painted and I drank coffee in the early morning sunlight, we chatted, discovering a mutual connection. I had found another new, old friend.

Seems he was a "reluctant messiah" of sorts. He had traveled the country over the years, staying in a spot as long as it felt right, collecting a bevy of occupations and experiences along the way. His forte was writing and he felt it was his time to share with the world what he had learned on his journey. A current vehicle was an eloquent children's book. It's premise, told through the character of an all-too-human rabbit, was that if you believe in yourself and your dreams, you can make them happen. We agreed to meet later that evening after I had toured the local wineries and experienced a mud bath, and he had completed his responsibilities for the day.

The evening was magical. Jack prepared an impressive gourmet appetizer, a skill acquired during a restaurant phase. I contributed a luscious bottle of cabernet sauvignon purchased at a favorite winery. After we listened to an audio tape of his book, he gifted me with an in-character reading from a rough-cut sequel. He had been working on it when I had initially seen him the night before.

After the reading he said he had a surprise. We walked along a dirt road toward the back of the resort, where I was asked to wait. Moments later I was standing within the dramatically shadowed majesty of an illuminated redwood grove. My mouth dropped in awe in response to the grand introduction. Shortly thereafter, we were plunged into darkness. Blown fuse. It was great while it lasted.

Since I had been raving about the food at the Italian restaurant we had both visited, we decided to regroup at the eatery's bar. We had a glorious time ordering appetizers, wines, cognac and dessert, speculating on the meaning of life while jesting with the wait staff and bartender. We promised to meet for another wonderful, celebratory dinner when his books were a major success.

The next morning on the Summer Solstice, fuzzy from the late night before, I left for the Avenue of the Giants, home of the colossal redwoods. What looked like a four-hour expressway drive by midwest map standards turned out to be a lumber truck dodge 'em game as I teetered on a two lane highway that snaked through the mountains. Seven hours later, I arrived in the miniscule town of Miranda where I gratefully rented a charming cabin spotted in a AAA guidebook. I was exhausted, stressed from the drive and had the uncomfortably vulnerable feeling that I was in the middle of a secluded nowhere, which I was, and apart from the cabin manager no one knew of my whereabouts, which was true.

Around four o'clock the next morning, I awakened with a jolt. Whatever uncomfortable feelings I had experienced the night before had escalated into a suffocating anxiety I hadn't felt in years. As 911 didn't appear to be an option in the area, I was thankful to have the skills to work through the distress and subsequently settle into a much needed sleep.

After discarding an overly-mayonnaised egg salad sandwich that was the afternoon version of breakfast in a two-building town, I set out to explore the Avenue of the Giants. I had a feeling of deep reverence as I silently padded through the primeval forests. Contemplating the amount of time the redwoods had maintained a sentinel stance was difficult to comprehend. I hiked, took photographs with my diligently acquired camera and laid at their feet.

I eventually made my way back to San Francisco via the coast. My initial desert plans to be open to receive information had not been a priority on my adventure. I had explored "in the moment" and considered my thousand mile journey into unfamiliar territory to be a vision quest.

You are infinitely safe.

I remember times when I was gripped with such uniden-tified fear, that I was afraid to go outside of my apartment. To have learned to trust "self" and "flow" enough to enjoy an unstructured adventure alone, was remarkably liberating. I realized that wherever I was, in whatever situation I was in, I had me, and that "me" was the consciousness that was eternal.

Chapter 19

I was talking with Merrill about my adventure when out of left field he broached the subject of my pendants. He stated that they had sparked dormant information which brought innate knowledge to consciousness. Great. It wasn't that I didn't appreciate what he was communicating on a mystical level, but income was kind of a necessity in 3-D land. I viewed the pendant experience from the baseline perspective of another project which had originated from the heart, but one that hadn't returned much of a free-flowing reward, actually, not even a trickle.

I knew the natural state of the universe was lavish abundance. Fruit trees didn't dole out their goods in metered fits and starts. They gave freely—some for harvest, some for the birds and animals, some to provide seeds to regenerate, some to fade back into the ground. Fruit trees didn't decide that one day they were on and the next day, "Ehh, don't think so." A belief I was generating was effluenting my affluence.

As I thought about this, apparitions of years past appeared and whispered in fear-laced contraction, "Can't afford it, too expensive, don't deserve it, no you can't, sorry, No." Apparitions of years present stated, "GNP, unemployment, downsizing, bottom line."

On the career front, working independently for years had provided me with the luxury of setting my own schedule which I had grown to appreciate. I had the ability to make what I considered to be good money on the projects I secured and the added bonus of enjoying the creative process to the point that time stopped. I once heard that when one loses track of time because they're so immersed in what they're doing, time actually does stop. Good way to stay young. I was also aware that being able to touch the space from where creativity emerged allowed me to tap into the missing ninety percent potential I was looking to retrieve years before.

So what was missing? Steady flow that would eliminate concern about flow. A Catch-22. I wanted freedom to create without financial concern—the free-flowing abundance the fruit trees so innocently demonstrated. They didn't think about it, it was their natural state. I longed to be a tree.

Later that month I drove to a relative's house to help with my sister's bridal shower. Being ten years younger, she was the first sibling to become engaged. Being single sometimes posed its challenges, particularly when I felt like Cinderella sweeping the floors instead of the Belle of the Ball. I worked through ambivalent feelings and was willing to help make it a pleasant occasion.

My sister and her fiancé were not actually attending because they lived in California—they were present by proxy. I made life-size photo images of their heads, mounted them on stakes (no malice intended, I swear), and planted them at the front door. Festooned with paper garlands, they greeted their guests.

In the process of scrambling to finish cleaning before company arrived (I wasn't kidding about the Cinderella thing), I lost my footing and skidded down a flight of carpeted stairs, banging my neck on the edges in the process. After recovering from the initial shock, I continued with my pre-party checklist.

During the festivities I retrieved my voice mail messages and discovered that I had inadvertently had a shower in Chicago which originated from my apartment. Pipes had backed up in the kitchen drowning the apartment below. The landlord was handling it; allegedly the situation was under control.

Later in the afternoon I was alerted by a visiting relative that a national magazine, which had recently been published by a long-time client, looked suspiciously close to design work I had done earlier for a similar project. I bristled. The same thing had been mentioned by an acquaintance I had seen at a party weeks before. I temporarily shelved the information and made a mental note to check it out once I returned home.

By the time I was packing to return to Chicago, I wasn't able to move my head. During each of three consequent visits to a chiropractor, I was sprayed with a localized numbing agent because any head movement extracted tears of pain. In addition to the current injury, x-rays revealed a lack of normal neck curvature—possibly the result of a head plant I had tumbled through while skiing on a Colorado double-diamond black run years before. The stair skid was almost fortunate because a previously unknown situation was detected which could have caused enormous problems in the long run. The doctor recommended ongoing corrective care.

It had been very hot and humid in the midwest the week I was detained. When I returned to my un-air-conditioned apartment, warped kitchen cabinets, moldy dish towels, and a multitude of ants swarmed to greet me hello. The kitchen was a disaster and whatever had been soaked days before had bacteria-baked for a week. I was overwhelmed with a useless kitchen, the scope of cleaning necessary to make it habitable, and the situation with my neck. On top of that, a design project I was engaged to work on within the week was with the same client who's actions were in question.

I had been aware for years that her approach to management involved fear-based manipulation and con-trol. Whatever lessons we had learned together over a decade-long history were winding down. I had grown from feeling intimidated to becoming amused. Even so, business interactions were an energy drain. With the latest confirmed information regarding "borrowing," I vacillated between higher perspective thoughts and moments of descension into feelings of betrayal. My goal with the rapidly upcoming project was to complete it as easily as possible, provide the client with a superior product and collect a significant paycheck in the end. Emotions would have to be put in abeyance for the time being.

One question remained. Would I eventually call her on her actions and risk losing the relationship which represented substantial income or let it go? Whichever way I went, our relationship was irretrievably altered. I was in a psychically acidic pickle and uncharacteristically belched throughout the duration of the project.

As I was lamenting my multiple situations to a friend, he said, "Do you think that m-a-y-b-e you're getting a message?" My time in The Emerald City was coming to a close.

*Some beings have
an underlying belief
that chaos
precedes change
and will inadvertently
create the events which
support that belief.*

For as much as I wanted change, taking the final steps
toward manifesting it gave me the willies. Fear of the
unknown, lack of trust in favorable outcome, and the
steps necessary to create it seemed overwhelming. It
would appear that I needed to have "in your face"
circumstances that left me little opportunity but to
reluctantly jump into a new arena. Once I did, I was
usually pleased. For the sake of ease and grace, however,
I needed to refine my approach.

Chapter **20**

**Ask yourself what brings
you joy.**

I picked up a rumpled copy of a local newspaper from
a recent trip to Michigan and began dialing realtors. It
was September. My goal was to move by the first of
December. It no longer made sense to endure living in
a place I didn't enjoy.

Realtors said it would be difficult to find an annual
rental in the area because owners capitalized on summer
resort rates which were prime. My landlord said I'd never
sublease my apartment by December because it was too
close to the holidays. He owned two large apartment
buildings and had years of experience to draw from.
Secure that the situation I wanted had been created,
I discounted their warnings and continued undaunted.

A few weeks later I received a call from a realtor
who said she and her husband owned a home they
would be willing to rent. A potential buyer's offer fell
through and it was available. When I saw the house,
I immediately liked it. It felt wonderful, was nearly new,
light, bright, beautifully appointed and had a huge deck
overlooking sand dunes. I told her I'd think about it,
buying time while my mind caught up with what had
been set into motion.

The kitchen situation resolved nicely. I received an
insurance check for damages and was able to have a
shower of my own at a fabulous home furnishings store.
It was wonderful to be able to stack beautiful replacement

merchandise on the counter and know it was paid for with an obligation-free check.

I found a talented chiropractor who didn't use oxymoronic cracking as a method for neck care. He was able to locate and correct an additional problem. My head wasn't aligned with my neck. The questionable phrase, "Your head isn't screwed on right" took on new meaning. When he moved it back into position, there was such a wonderful release, I simultaneously laughed and cried. The doctor, an intuitive healer, said he felt I'd been waiting for that adjustment for a long time and predicted my life wouldn't continue to be the struggle it had usually been.

The dreaded design project was completed without casualties and a congratulatory call was received on the excellent product that had been created and produced. I processed feelings about the underlying situation, but still wasn't sure how to handle it because of the potential for an upcoming project months down the road. Although I intellectually knew clients weren't the source of income, merely a channel, I was skittish about burning bridges. There had to be a win-win approach to the situation--I just didn't know what it was. I continued to work on the "borrowing predicament" from within and refrained from any outer action for the time being.

A call was placed to the realtor to let her know I was interested in her house, however, I wasn't comfortable signing a new lease until my apartment had been sub-leased. We agreed to talk in a month when I'd returned from course-related traveling. On a superficial level I realized I was taking a chance that the house wouldn't be available. On another level, I had created moving by

December and knew this was where I would be. Focus needed to remain with that thought.

In the meantime I went to an idyllic farm in Wisconsin to teach in the midst of autumn colors. I found it a joy and privilege to assist students in untangling themselves from what they thought were their own "givens" to emerge into a limitless world. From there I flew to Florida to receive advanced training for instructors.

When something ceases
to bring you joy,
you always have
the option
to change it.

When I finally realized that I deserved to enjoy my life, despite of a long list of judgments regarding responsible behavior, situations and circumstances began to change—quickly.

Chapter **21**

You don't need a crowbar.

Being with friends who shared the same knowledge had its pluses and minuses. Basically, this meant I was called on the carpet if I found myself whining about anything in my life. Self-responsibility was great . . . sometimes. Well, most of the time, anyway.

After hours, my course roommate and I continued to work and play through our own issues. It was the end of October and if I was really going to liberate myself from Chicago, I had thirty days to find a landlord-approved sub-lessee for my apartment, confirm the house in Michigan and relocate. I was facing a lot of unknowns. Apart from the physical mechanics of moving, there was the question of clients. What would happen to my business? The "what ifs" swarmed like the aftermath of an upended hornet's nest.

By the time I returned home, my intention was clear. I didn't know how everything was going to come about, but I was sure it would.

A tenant was found the first week back. Lease negotiations on the house resolved simply and easily. I was in a state of mind where I wasn't concerned about clients. I'd create what was needed after I settled in. A reasonably priced mover was available and booked a week ahead of schedule, Thanksgiving Eve. The only glitch was dealing with a web of phone company customer service reps who plead "the fifth" in my attempts to cancel, transfer and establish new service between two states. But what would a move be without a little aggravation for drama?

Chicago was left as unceremoniously as it had been entered. I had arrived in the back seat of my parent's Kingswood Estate station wagon, the back of which contained my life's possessions. I left, driving Craig's mother's old Pontiac, which had a fabric ceiling liner that draped like a Bedouin tent. Craig drove my car (by now a domestic model) because I was reacting to exhaust smells in the cabin which caused discomfort to the point of nausea. Possessions were somewhere on I-94 in a Ryder Truck. I was an overwrought, crying mess.

The movers were late, having taken a wrong turn that took them halfway through Indiana. Craig stayed with me until they arrived, leaving shortly thereafter to pick up his daughter for their regular weekend visit. Once the boxes and furniture were deposited, I went to a local Chinese restaurant and brought back a carton of won ton soup. I hadn't been able to eat for days having been busy with packing, cleaning and the emotions of impending uprootedness. I planned to open a bottle of cabernet in celebration of my accomplishment after I had taken in some food.

When my neighbor called with greetings and asked if anything was needed, I was rummaging through boxes looking for a phantom cork screw. She and her husband extended an invitation to share a pre-holiday, welcome home glass of wine. Hours later, I stumbled across the leaf-covered distance that spanned our houses, miraculously located a sheet and released into sleep.

Intention
moves mountains.

Enough said.

Chapter 22

The new location was wonderful. Instead of looking out from a bedroom/office window and seeing a 1940's brick courtyard, I had an office that faced a small pond, woods and a beautiful white pine. Sometimes deer passed by. Living in a house was wonderful, too. It was the first time I hadn't shared walls with anyone since leaving home at age seventeen. There was one stop light within a twenty mile stretch of main road and being off-season, it was rare to see another car by nightfall. The air was clean and the only machinated sound in the area was from the soothing rumble and whistle of trains that moved through nearby tracks.

Time was an interesting factor in the area due to the geographic proximity of the region to a tri-state area. Michigan is on eastern time. It's close to Chicago which is on central time. It's closer to Indiana which is on eastern and central time depending on what county you're in. Throw in a little "Spring Forward, Fall Back" daylight savings action and things really got interesting.

Having been situated in a home office for years, I had grown accustomed to creating my own schedule which accommodated internal rhythms. I wasn't clock based. Eating, sleeping, working and relaxing were based on internal cues rather than contrived time dictates. I had the awareness that time itself was an organizational, linear framework that was collectively chosen, unconsciously or otherwise, to abide by. Truth is, it didn't really exist. It was merely an idea.

In keeping with functioning within the framework, I set the stove clock to eastern time and the microwave clock to central time. Somewhere between Spring Forward, Fall Back, eastern versus central, and repairs that interrupted whatever time 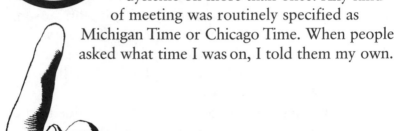 was set anyway, I gave up on the clock in the car. Scheduling calculations for appointments between zones some-times became an exercise in mental gymnastics, one I admit to going dyslexic on more than once. Any kind of meeting was routinely specified as Michigan Time or Chicago Time. When people asked what time I was on, I told them my own.

*Time and space
are relative to your
own perceptions.*

When I was initially self-employed, I felt guilty about
not following a traditional nine to five routine. To be
valid, I thought I should have the same structure that
"legitimate" business people followed. As I let go of that
judgment, I began to feel my own rhythms. It was then
that it became easy to see the framework for what it was.

Chapter 23

Trust your knowing.

Part of the information I had received in one of my earlier chats with other aspects of consciousness involved forming a foundation with the purpose of assisting in bringing more light and awareness to the planet.

With unadmitted, self-important flair, part of my original plan to go to the desert was for the purpose of receiving more white knight input. Very Jesus like. I envisioned building a physical organization in the linear manner of a, b, c. As incoming (INCOMING!) messages grew increasingly repetitive and vague, I became frustrated with the process of tapping into something that didn't seem to offer new information or an action-based plan for moving forward. I eventually tuned out and focused on routine tasks at hand. I realized I had been looking outside myself for guidance—no one said inter-dimensional sources necessarily had their acts together.

For all my years of self-reliance, I had inadvertently fallen into the sometime seductive trap that someone or something wiser, stronger, more aware would, could, should call the shots. Even if I chose to blindly follow directives, it would be infinitely more empowering to know that that's what I intentionally chose to do rather than be unconsciously swept along. Within the mystery and gift of newfound communication abilities, I had lost sight of the basics. I later had confirmation from origins which will remain unnamed that I had mined the gem that deliberately garbled messages had hidden. Think for yourself! Oy.

Given my relatively recent experience, it was with a very large grain of salt that I planned to attend a gathering that was to include channeled information. Since I was in the mood for company I went, despite the evening's slated program.

Surprisingly, the message echoed the familiar concept that what you believe is what you'll experience, so you may as well create what you want. Life is a playground, not a knuckle-slapping schoolroom. I certainly was in alignment with that. I hadn't moved to a resort area with the idea of suffering.

My feeling was that suffering was a neat little trick instilled into the collective consciousness like the time framework. It provided structure and control. A joyful society was one that spawned independent thinkers. Or was it the other way around? No matter, hard to control, those independent thinkers. Can't have people walking around doing what they want and happy. What kind of world would it be?

"Okay, so let's come up with a plan that'll quash any semblance of joy. We'll create the ideas of scarcity, aging, sickness, fear, and death. And to cork a really obvious ticket through, we'll definitely have to slam dunk the divinity out of physical love. For good measure let's throw in that they're spinning out in their own misery, an insignificant speck on an unyielding tread!"

"Yeah, we've got 'em licked. They'll never get outta that."

*There is no greater
authority than
your own
knowingness.*

I secretly wanted someone else to take control of my life,
because sorting through the expanse of options available
in any given moment felt overwhelming. When I eventually made the shift from wanting someone to tell me what
to do to feeling what was right from within, I instinctively
knew which choices to make. It was the most basic, yet
pivotal awareness—learning to trust what I already knew.

Chapter **24**

The heart connection.

A few months after moving, I was looking out from the window that faced the dunes as I drank an early morning cup of coffee. I was immediately aware that light beings were perceptible in a line that ran parallel to the deck. A quick inventory revealed they completely encircled the house. When I telepathically asked what was going on, they said they were there to protect me. "Why?" I thought. "There's nothing going on here." I was puzzled, but continued with the day, periodically checking to "see" if they were still around. They were.

My friend, Rex, called during the afternoon to say he had unexpectedly received $200 a plate tickets for a benefit that evening at the Drake Hotel in Chicago. It was black tie, a table needed to be filled, would I like to join him. The hotel was legendary—I jumped at the opportunity.

The event was a pleasant break from routine. Once it concluded, the group from our table decided to prolong the festivities by stopping at a local jazz club. After several dances, I left the city to return home. It was shortly after midnight.

An hour and a half later my car was suddenly side-slipping toward a deep ditch on the right-hand side of the expressway. Ice had appeared out of nowhere. I managed to avoid the ditch, but the car careened wildly out of control on a tractionless surface. I braced myself as it spun across three lanes of traffic hitting a concrete median several times before coming to an abrupt stop. The car landed facing opposite traffic flow. Once I caught my breath and realized I couldn't open the front doors, I maneuvered out a back door to see where the car had hit, hoping for minor damage. No such luck.

I was able to start the car and eventually limped it along the shoulder of the expressway toward the flashing lights of a police car a mile or so ahead. Trying not to slip on the ice in three-inch heels, I approached the squad car which flanked a jackknifed semi in the ditch. After a brief exchange regarding the treacherous road conditions, a tow truck was summoned as I filled out requisite forms.

When the driver suggested the car be taken to his repair facility, I started to cry. I had held it together while details needed to be handled, but suddenly the impact of what had happened started to affect me. It was nearly three in the morning and I was cold, tired, and felt very vulnerable. Fighting back tears, I jabbered in free fall delivery that I-only-lived-five-miles-away-and-couldn't-I-just-drive-the-car-home-if-they-fixed-the-flat-tires-because-there-was-no-one-at-home-there-was-no-one-in-the-area-I-could-call-I-was-in-the-middle-of-nowhere-and-I-was-alone. The driver gently suggested that the car needed to go to the shop for insurance purposes, but he would be happy to take me home. As I sat in his truck and watched the car being put on the lift, "We're here to protect you," registered in my mind. It was then that I realized I could have easily been killed or seriously injured. I was humbled and overwhelmed that I had indeed been protected and sobbed with recognition.

Several days later my neighbor passed my office window as she walked her dog. We were exchanging morning pleasantries when she asked where my car was. When I related what had happened, she shared something very interesting. On her way to work, days before, a song she hadn't previously heard played on the radio. The lyrics included the words "angels among us." She had been moved to tears to the point of needing to reapply her make-up. It was the same morning the light beings had appeared.

*For every degree you
open your heart,
you profoundly affect
all that is.*

When I risked vulnerability and ridicule by sharing something private and very special that wasn't considered
"mainstream," I found a beautiful connection point.
Had I not spoken my truth, I would not have heard
another's truth. This sharing allowed the unmistakable
realization that our individual experiences, although
framed differently, were poignantly connected.

Chapter **25**

Oops!

The immediate environment provided many reflections. There was a large maple tree in the yard that had several birdfeeders hanging from it, which a plethora of birds used as feeding stations. I quickly found out how voraciously they, and a few resident squirrels, went through seed. Although grocery store outings now regularly included food for my outdoor pets, I gladly kept the feeders stocked. The locals were a continuing source of entertainment.

Since the tree was at a slight distance from the house and I wanted to watch the birds and squirrels more closely, bowls of seed were moved onto the deck where I could see them from the kitchen table. Dramas worthy of the best daytime television played out. Although there was an abundance of food, whichever bird had first claimed its spot on the pile fiercely defended its territory by making threatening pecks to perceived invaders. I found myself saying out loud, "Come on you guys, there's plenty. Why don't you just share?"

I reflected on their actions. . . how many times had I done the same thing? If I was going to be brutally honest, was I, through years of inner evolvement, all that different from those tiny birds?

Of course I wished everyone well at face value. But what about the twinges. . . deliriously happy newlyweds, serial-murderer lottery winners, obnoxious sports types with gazillion dollar salaries. . . the things that really hit my buttons. Was I immune? Not exactly, but I was working on it. I saw a quote from Taoism which I clipped out and resolutely stuck on the refrigerator with a magnet. "Regard your neighbor's gain as your own gain, and your neighbor's loss as your own loss." I knew there was something in it for me—I cringed when I read it.

A friend had visited on a winter afternoon and seeing that the feeders were empty, filled them. And I mean *filled* them. There was a mound of seed rising from the bottom of a mini, gazebo-like feeder that rivaled the sand dunes. Since it was devoured as quickly as it was put out, I usually replenished the feeder moderately to extend time between trips for more food. He had lavishly given them the last contents of a thirty pound bag.

At first I was slightly annoyed, but when I saw the birds sitting in the enormous pile, leisurely eating *together*, I knew there was another metaphor. Why would I meter out food when the supply was endless? Okay, so it involved a trip to the store. So what?

Perhaps the way I dealt with the bird food was the way I treated myself. Having lived with roller coaster income for years, didn't I have the belief that resources were to be conserved? Didn't I carefully consider nearly every purchase I made, usually looking for sales? There was another sting of recognition. How would the unlimited abundance that was inherent in the universe come to me if I had my own system of checks and balances? What if I opened myself without concern, much the way my friend had dumped the mountain of seed which the birds were thoroughly enjoying? It felt much better to be open and allowing rather than contracted and in fear.

My outdoor pets continued to test me. Since becoming familiar with food on the deck, if I was inadvertently lapse in getting birdseed into the terra cotta flower pot trays that doubled as their bowls, they took it upon themselves to go to the source. Several enormous bird food bags had been shredded, scattering paper and seed over the deck. I played a game with myself. If I could see the aftermath of their antics and not think of them as seed-grubbing varmints, I knew I had mastered the abundance issue with flying colors.

When you focus
on "have,"
you create the opportunity
for "more."

When I wrote this chapter, I was so focused on equating
the concept of abundance with cash flow that I lost sight
of the incredible riches that continually grace me. Abundance comes in many forms. I was incredibly gifted within
the categories of friends, family, health, environment,
laughter, awareness, abilities, personal freedom, and the
capacity to feel (for starters). I had temporarily forgotten
that the concept includes much more than money. Duh.

Chapter 26

I was introduced to a person who was affectionately
referred to as JohnTwo. Reason being, he was a walk-in.
Having fulfilled his life's contract, JohnOne, whom I never
met, made the decision to leave his body which allowed
JohnTwo (by mutual agreement) to assume JohnOne's
physical form. In a story superceding the intrigue of the
best of sci-fi thrillers, JohnTwo had come from a distant
universe as a benevolent teacher. For real.

Although it was the first time I had knowingly met
a walk-in, it wasn't the first time I'd heard of the concept.
The talk at the Field Museum had broached the subject
of undetected aliens among us. I had heard third party
accounts of someone knowing someone who was reportedly from elsewhere.

Years before the prediction had been made regarding
an increase in alien-laced media programming as preparation for events to come. I was astounded by the explosive
number of television programs that had alien themes or
star (no pun intended) characters. Reference to the
subject was routine. I now understood how this was
originating—channeled information and walk-ins.

Earth was big news from a universal perspective. I had
heard it compared to *People* magazine's cover story of
the year. We're embarking upon unprecedented waters;
moving into an era of tolerance, compassion and love for
one another despite the illusion of perceived differences

and resultant violence. It had never been done before. What would transpire would literally affect all that is. Each and every one of us was here for a front-row seat by specific choice whether consciously aware of it or not.

We had an audience. We also had assistance. As in JohnTwo's case, not only had he come to experience events, but to assist in the transformation, as many of us had, by his awareness, presence and guidance. We're on deck for spectacular times.

Pop!

Party on.

This is self-explanatory.

Chapter **27**

One more thing.

Family relationships were sometimes a great challenge. I was in a particularly trying phase when I received a phone call from my sister. My brother was giving a talk about his life within the context of a personal growth retreat. Organizers had requested that family members write loving letters to participants which would be read over the course of the weekend.

I groaned. The last time we had spoken, my brother lashed into a mental meltdown tirade that left me holding the phone a foot away from my ear. He had left apologetic messages on my answering machine, but was the last person I wanted to speak to, let alone write a glowing letter about.

The satirical nature of the situation was noted. I'd just have to push through some Grade A emotional concrete to get to the point of picking up a pen. Eventually, I decided to focus on an experience we'd had weeks before:

Recently I experienced a sweet moment with my brother when he and my sister unexpectedly decided to stay overnight at my house near Lake Michigan. When I awakened the morning after their arrival and raised the shades, I was greeted with an unexpected fairyland of winter splendor. I hadn't seen lake effect snow like that all year. Eight inches of fresh powder clung in delicate balance to the trees in the woods that surrounded the house.

We watched the birds at the feeders in the yard and marveled at the beauty of the snow which continued to fall. As we continued watching in the early morning light, a hawk unexpectedly descended upon a cardinal which subsequently scattered the feeding birds. The hawk flew away with the cardinal in its clutches. My brother and sister went outside to examine the cardinal's point of departure — nothing was left except feathers in the snow.

I joined them outside where we took pictures to commemorate the snowfall. Instead of returning to the house, I told my brother I wanted to walk to a nearby stand of pines. When we reached the grove, he gently kicked the trunk of a tree releasing an avalanche of snow. I laughed with the sheer joy of it. Continuing with our game, he'd point to a tree and I'd stand under it looking up as small clumps of descending snow gave way to a gentle woosh of white which fanned out with a wind as it reached the ground.

During that brief time, veils were lifted. I was in the eternal moment enjoying an incredible experience with my brother from a space apart from the familiar identities of family-past.

They left to return home shortly

thereafter. By then the snow had stopped falling and the winds had come laying bare the branches that had been so lavishly embellished an hour before. Carpe diem, sieze the moment, felt incomplete. Embrace the moment in the moment felt more true.

That evening, as I walked through the stand of pines in the darkness, I remembered the joy of the morning. When the moon reflected familiar footprints, I was struck with tenderness for the being I call my brother. So I'll embrace the moment and tell him, tell you, I love you.

When I had chosen to push beyond my judgments regarding the phone experience with my brother and focus on what was special between us, I touched the loving space that was there all along. It was like cracking out of the darkness of a walnut shell and being exposed to brilliant sunlight, much like the white-light experience of a decade before.

I realized that when I addressed the challenging situations that were presented in my own life in a loving, self-responsible manner, I, in turn, positively affected the world around me. It was a tiny step by tiny step process that, when multiplied by many others, had truly grand ramifications for the planet.

I also had the revelation that those who had touched my life, in all their varying roles, had ultimately appeared to best serve my growth, and I, theirs. It was as if we wore costumes. Okay, you'll be this and I'll be that and we'll have this really amazing situation together, and then we'll take off the costumes and laugh about what a good time we had. Despite outer appearances, beyond the limits of personality and the heavily draped stage, the basis was ultimately love. And the curtain was indeed lifting.

A snowflake present from an
earthbound star child, Rachel, age six.

*Heaven on Earth
is entirely within your realm
of possibility.*

Scout's Honor.

Epilogue

When a one-time settlement offer was proposed for my
legal matter, I was personally insulted and adamantly
opposed. From that viewpoint I was also lost in the
illusion and feeling drowned in negativity. Knowing a
higher aspect of self had created the very situation I so
vehemently opposed, I decided it was time to integrate
what had been learned and move on.

In introspective celebration, I burned the contents of
the cardboard box that contained five years of files, five
years of attention and energy. It was cathartic to finally
unburden myself from a pervasive millstone to make
room for experiences that are consistent with who I am
in the moment.

I began this book with The Quest for my own
version of the Holy Grail. Searching out the ordinary
pursuits of money and relationship catapulted me onto
a journey I didn't consciously want, yet at the same time
propelled me far beyond my wildest, most fulfilling
dreams. In true Arthurian, Ruby Slipper fashion, I now
know the answer lies within.

I once looked for external validation because I felt
I had little value. Invariably being guided to return within,
an unfoldment prevailed along an ever-ascending spiral.
Somewhere along the spiral I learned to appreciate myself. It was then that the wonder of the universe became
evident and I learned to play with its magic.

I now know that my higher self is a loving and benevolent ally that is ultimately interested in guiding my highest destiny. "Battle Axe" served its purpose. It joyfully no longer applies.

With great love, respect and honor for you and Your Journey,

Cats

Appendix

1. The use of MariEL® energy for physical, mental, emotional, and spiritual healing, began in 1983 through the attunement of many thousands of practitioners throughout the United States, Canada and Europe. In addition to the expedition of healing, MariEL balances the male and female energy within the individual. It also balanced the energy of the planet. In 1995 the attunements of practitioners ceased because MariEL had completed its divine mission, which was to anchor feminine energy onto the earth plane.

2. Avatar® is a fascinating nine-day course based upon the observation that what you believe will cause you to create, or attract, the experiences you call "your life." From the expanded awareness gained through the course, you gain the ability to identify and change limiting beliefs. By deliberately choosing new, empowering beliefs, you create your new reality. The awareness and mental tools acquired on the Avatar course are yours to use for life.

The worldwide mission of Avatar is to contribute to personal transcendence and an enlightened planetary civilization. Ten of thousands of people have taken the course since its inception in 1987; Avatar is delivered in over fifty countries throughout the world. For more information call 1-888-4-AVATAR.

About the Author: In addition to writing, designing and other creative endeavors, Catherine Lenard is a transformational educator. She is committed to healing through personal evolvement and the expansion of consciousness on the planet and elsewhere.

Correspondence may be directed through the publisher:

YOUR HAND'S IN THE INC.

P. O. Box 65
Lakeside, Michigan 49116 U.S.A.

Order Form

Telephone or fax orders: 1-888-693-BOOK (U.S. & Canada, toll free. International calls: +1-219-879-8998). Have your VISA or MasterCard ready with number and expiration date.

Postal orders: Your Hand's in the Inc., P.O. Box 65, Lakeside, Michigan, 49116 U.S.A.

Please send a copy of *All I Ever Wanted Was A Lot of Money and A Husband; Instead I Got Enlightenment* to:

_____

Name (please print clearly)

_____

Address (include apartment number if applicable)

_____

City   *State/Province*   *Zip/Post Code*

_____

Country   *Phone: country code-area code-local number*

Shipping: *U.S. orders*—add $2 for shipping. Allow two weeks for delivery. ($4 for Priority Mail; allow one week for delivery). Michigan orders add 6% (.72c) sales tax. *Canadian orders*—add $5 for shipping. Allow two weeks for delivery. *International orders*— add $7 for shipping. Allow three weeks for delivery.

Payment:

check   _____   *Canadian or International orders:* U.S. Currency money order or bank check.

credit card _____   (VISA _____ MasterCard _____)

_____

Name on card (please print clearly)

_____-_____-_____-_____

Card Number

_____

Expiration Date

_____

Signature

Total:

Book: $11.95c

Sales Tax:
(Michigan only)   .72c

Shipping: _____

Total: $U.S._____